WILD OCEAN

Who's watching whom? A young sea lion and a young terrestrial primate meet in a wild ocean.

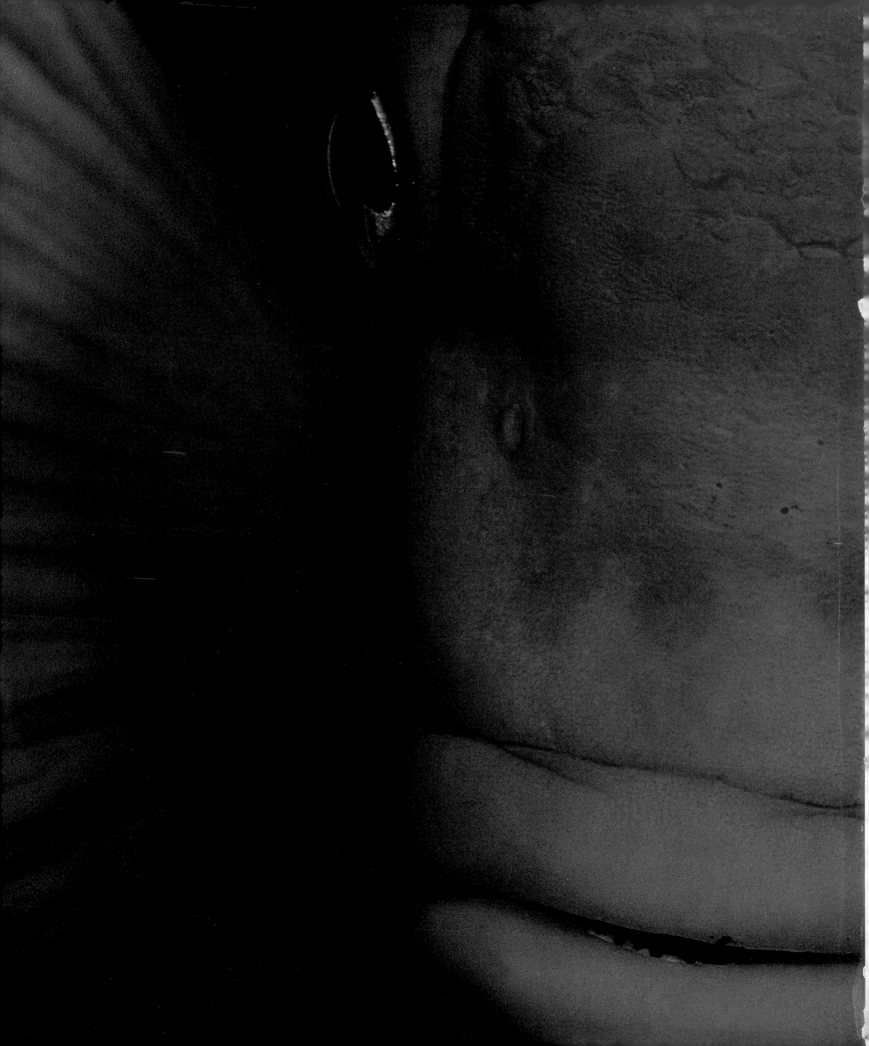

WILD OCEAN

AMERICA'S PARKS UNDER THE SEA

BY SYLVIA A. EARLE AND WOLCOTT HENRY

NATIONAL GEOGRAPHIC

WASHINGTON, D.C.

CONTENTS

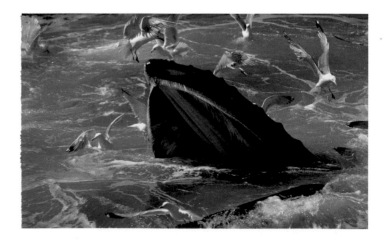

PRECEDING PAGES: *In a face-to-face encounter with California's state marine fish, the garibaldi, you can meet eight ounces of high-energy action.*

FOREWORD

IN JUNE 1998, on a windy bluff overlooking Monterey Bay, President Clinton and I joined hundreds of other Americans in rededicating our nation to the protection of a resource as vital as it is vast: our oceans. The National Ocean Conference was a historic gathering, drawing together for the first time the full array of ocean interests, from government to industry, science to conservation. New measures launched that day will help restore coastal reefs, rebuild fisheries, enhance the competitiveness of America's ports, and guard our shores against catastrophic oil spills. But there was consensus among participants that if we truly are to protect our oceans, we must better understand them.

That is the goal of another new initiative celebrated that day in Monterey: the Sustainable Seas Expeditions. This extraordinary partnership of the National Geographic Society and the National Oceanic and Atmospheric Administration, with support from the Richard and Rhoda Goldman Fund, will explore as never before America's most precious ocean environments: our 12 national marine sanctuaries.

The designation of our first national marine sanctuary in 1975—the resting place of the U.S.S. *Monitor,* off Cape Hatteras—was an act as momentous and visionary as the creation of our first national park a century earlier. From the kelp forests and humpback whales of the Olympic Coast Sanctuary to the coral reefs and endangered loggerheads of the Florida Keys, these underwater reserves are the crown jewels of our marine endowment. These 18,000 square miles of American coastal waters harbor not only biological and geological diversity to rival Yellowstone or the Grand Canyon, but also irreplaceable fragments of our history and cultural heritage.

Like the national parks, the marine sanctuaries are places open for the enjoyment of every American. The five-year Sustainable Seas Expeditions, led by famed ocean explorer and National Geographic Explorer-in-Residence Sylvia Earle and former National Marine Sanctuary Program director Francesca Cava, will explore, study, and document America's "parks under the sea" so that we can better protect them. For those not making the journey, and for those who wish to plan one, *Wild Ocean* offers a stunning introduction to these 12 watery worlds still largely uncharted—a glimpse of the wonders awaiting our discovery. For ages, the seas have been a source of sustenance, solace, mystery, and awe. Together, we can ensure that they are all this, and more, for generations yet to come.

Al Gore

AL GORE

VICE PRESIDENT, UNITED STATES OF AMERICA

From face mask, snorkel, and flippers, to scuba gear, it is possible for almost anyone to meet creatures, such as this California sea hare, on their own terms, underwater.

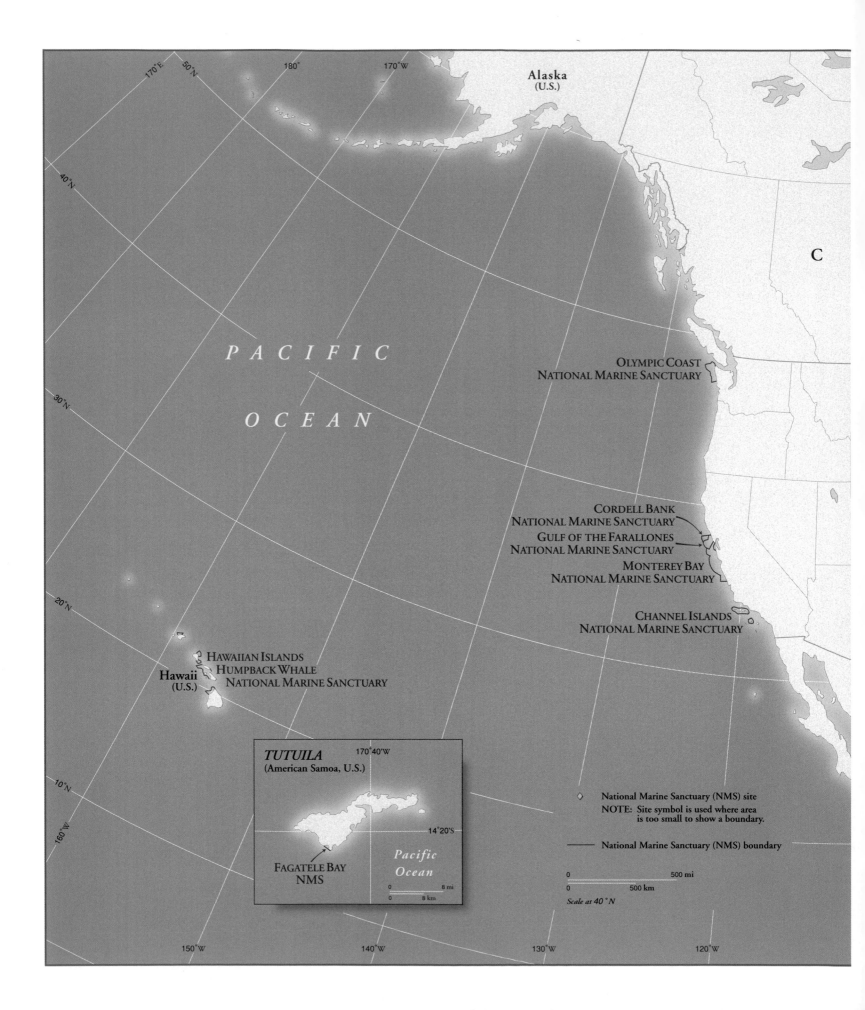

Alaska
(U.S.)

C

PACIFIC

OCEAN

OLYMPIC COAST
NATIONAL MARINE SANCTUARY

CORDELL BANK
NATIONAL MARINE SANCTUARY

GULF OF THE FARALLONES
NATIONAL MARINE SANCTUARY

MONTEREY BAY
NATIONAL MARINE SANCTUARY

CHANNEL ISLANDS
NATIONAL MARINE SANCTUARY

HAWAIIAN ISLANDS
HUMPBACK WHALE
NATIONAL MARINE SANCTUARY

Hawaii
(U.S.)

TUTUILA
(American Samoa, U.S.)

170°40'W

14°20'S

FAGATELE BAY
NMS

*Pacific
Ocean*

0   8 mi

0   8 km

◇ National Marine Sanctuary (NMS) site

NOTE: Site symbol is used where area
        is too small to show a boundary.

── National Marine Sanctuary (NMS) boundary

0   500 mi

0   500 km

Scale at 40° N

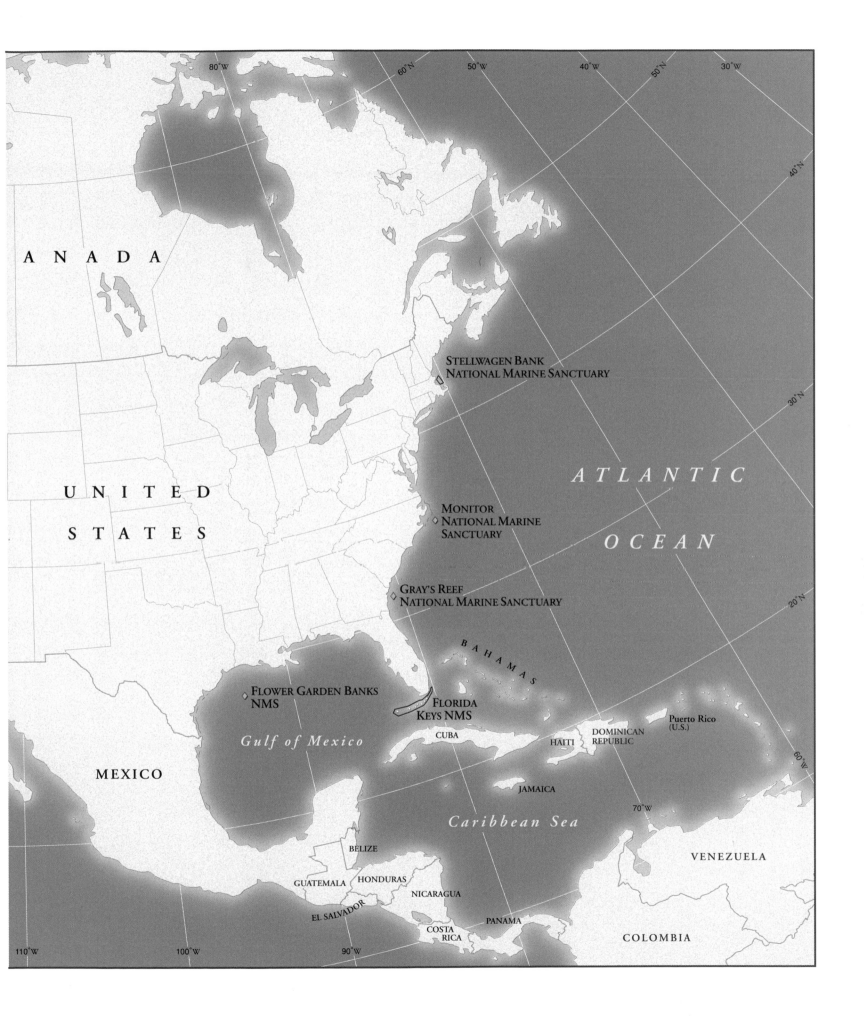

STELLWAGEN BANK
NATIONAL MARINE SANCTUARY

MONITOR
NATIONAL MARINE
SANCTUARY

GRAY'S REEF
NATIONAL MARINE SANCTUARY

ATLANTIC

OCEAN

B A H A M A S

FLOWER GARDEN BANKS
NMS

FLORIDA
KEYS NMS

Gulf of Mexico

CUBA

DOMINICAN
REPUBLIC

Puerto Rico
(U.S.)

HAITI

MEXICO

JAMAICA

Caribbean Sea

VENEZUELA

BELIZE

GUATEMALA   HONDURAS

NICARAGUA

EL SALVADOR

COSTA
RICA

PANAMA

COLOMBIA

A N A D A

U N I T E D

S T A T E S

80°W

60°N

50°W

40°W

50°N

30°W

40°N

30°N

20°N

110°W

100°W

90°W

70°W

60°W

OURS TO ENJOY

INTRODUCTION

BY SYLVIA EARLE

"I love you," I whispered into the ear of the ocean.
"Ever since I've known you,
I've loved you. I must see all your marvels, know all your beauty...."
And the ocean listened and snuggled closer to me.

HANS HASS
DIVING TO ADVENTURE

———————————

THINK OF WHAT IT IS LIKE to stand at the edge of a cliff surrounded by blue sky, watching birds ride that ocean of air with ease. Imagine gazing downward, wishing to lift off yourself, to skim over craggy peaks and the tips of trees, then glide to places beyond. In the sea, this is what I do; it is what anyone can do. My mother at 81 years for the first time donned a face mask and gently entered the clear atmosphere of water surrounding a tropical reef, where sea and sky seemed to merge as one; she floated weightlessly over branches of coral, met parrotfish face to face, watched crabs clambering through cathedrals of lavender sponges, marveled at skeins of fish glittering like bits of stained glass. "Why did I wait so long?" she mused. "I have lived by the sea most of my life, but never dreamed it was like this."

All of humankind has waited a long time—until about the middle of the 20th century—to begin to know the sea as birds know the sky. After all, by nature we are terrestrial, air-breathing mammals. We're designed by nature to walk, run, and climb, and with today's technologies it is possible for almost anyone to travel almost anywhere on the planet's surface and even to leave our own atmosphere for brief excursions into space. Much has been learned about the ocean from ships as well as from observations made high in the sky. But ironically, only a fraction of one percent of the sea below about

PRECEDING PAGES: *Millions have discovered what photographer*
Norbert Wu has: "There is nothing more fulfilling than swimming effortlessly
through a colorful coral reef and languidly hovering in crystal-clear waters."

a hundred feet has been visited even once by any human. Ed Cassano, Superintendent of the Channel Islands National Marine Sanctuary, observes, "For most of us, the ocean is seen from the beach, stretching to the horizon as a vast, uniform, dimensionless surface, which more often mirrors the sky than reveals what is below."

However, innovative new approaches to diving, ranging from masks, fins, and snorkels to creatively engineered deep-diving submersibles, passenger submarines, and a growing array of sensors and robotic devices now give us unprecedented new access to—and insight about—the ocean. As a new millennium begins, we have attained a turning point in terms of knowing—and caring—about the ocean that sustains us.

The oceans are a great metaphor—everything we do on land ends up in our coastal waters….The oceans mirror the health of our planet.

TED DANSON
PRESIDENT, AMERICAN OCEANS CAMPAIGN

Like my mother, Ed Cassano succumbed to the lure of the sea. He describes what it is like to "take the plunge" just offshore from his home in Santa Barbara, California: "Imagine being able to fly through a forest of trees a hundred feet high, unencumbered by gravity, to encounter dozens of species of birds and other animals in close proximity…. As I move along, I am joined by a group of sea lions who dart among the kelp with a grace and athletic ability that the world's greatest ballet dancers would envy. They dance away…while hundreds of fish move in and around the kelp fronds like songbirds in slow motion."

Many people in recent times have begun to explore the ocean on their own, whether by diving in as millions now do, or enjoying the view vicariously through the eyes, cameras, and recorders of those who bring back sights and sounds to share. Among the most important new awareness gained in decades of stunning discoveries about the ocean is that it is a living system, filled with small, medium, and sometimes very large creatures, from the sunniest of surface waters to the greatest, darkest depths, seven miles down. Most of Earth's water—97 percent—is in the sea, and, since water is vital for life, it is not surprising that about 97 percent of the space where life occurs, the so-called "biosphere," is ocean. We now know that the sea drives climate and weather, regulates and stabilizes the planet's temperature, generates more than 70 percent of the oxygen in the atmosphere, absorbs much of the carbon dioxide that is generated, and otherwise shapes planetary chemistry. The links among land, air, and sea have also come into focus, with the sea clearly the cornerstone of what makes life on Earth possible. Without it, this planet would be as barren and inhospitable as the moon or Mars.

Tantalizing new discoveries in America's aquatic backyard have inspired new ways of looking at the ocean, and new appreciation of how much more remains to be explored. Ancient submerged shorelines have been detected in the coastal areas offshore from Boston, Savannah, Miami, Galveston, San Francisco, Seattle, and elsewhere that provide clues to what North America was like before the end of the last ice age, when the sea level was much lower than now. Just recently, scientists found bones of woolly mammoths, saber-toothed cats, and other long-gone creatures of the Pleistocene epoch, 17 miles east of Sapelo Island, Georgia, and 60 feet underwater.

Discoveries about that "other America"—the submerged part of the country extending from the shore to the edge of the Exclusive Economic Zone some 200 miles seaward—include previously unknown ecosystems and forms of life, such as "ice worms" that live in frozen gas hydrates in the northern Gulf of Mexico. Hundreds of shipwrecks await exploration. There are also signs of trouble: declining populations of commercially exploited fish and other marine life, shoreline destruction, and growing pollution. While inspired by the promise of what else may be out there, down there, to help us understand the past and guide the future, there is also a growing sense of urgency about protecting the wild ocean as something too valuable to allow to be harmed.

Cousteau said it first, "If the ocean dies, we die."
To keep that from happening we need a better understanding of the ocean.

Scott Carpenter
Astronaut/Aquanaut

In 1998, the National Geographic Society embarked on an exciting new mission, the Sustainable Seas Expeditions, to explore, conduct research, and promote conservation and education of this vast, unknown part of North America. Developed in cooperation with the National Oceanic and Atmospheric Administration (NOAA), with support from the Richard and Rhoda Goldman Fund and the help of many governmental agencies, private institutions, corporations, and numerous scientists, engineers, policymakers, and educators, the expeditions will focus on America's system of National Marine Sanctuaries, a young but promising aquatic counterpart to the National Park System. I shall lead the expeditions, and Francesca Cava, former head of the National Marine Sanctuary Program, will serve as project manager.

When the National Park Service officially began in 1916, Congress ordered it by law to "promote and regulate the use" of the parks in conformity with their fundamental purpose: "to conserve the scenery and the natural and historic objects and the wildlife therein and to provide for the enjoyment of the same in such manner... as will leave them unimpaired for the enjoyment of future generations." Administered by the Department of the Interior, the service now oversees 378 national parks, monuments, historic sites and parks, battlefields, recreation areas, seashores and rivers, parkways, trails, and preserves. More than 60 of these areas have unique underwater historical or biological attractions, some 24 have marine resources, and several share boundaries with national marine sanctuaries. Complementing these protected areas are local- and state-managed marine parks and preserves. The windows they provide to our past and the protection they afford our future are incomparable. However, not until 1972, exactly a hundred years after the first national park was established, was action taken to authorize the designation of full-fledged national marine sanctuaries.

The creation of our national marine sanctuaries is a bold first step in the preservation of the natural wonders beneath the sea.

DR. ROBERT D. BALLARD
PRESIDENT, INSTITUTE FOR EXPLORATION

Through the National Marine Sanctuaries Act, NOAA, in the U.S. Department of Commerce, was named to manage the marine sanctuaries. They are defined as "areas of special national significance due to their resource or human use values" with special reference to "conservation, recreational, ecological, historic, research, educational or aesthetic value...." As of 1999, there are 12 sanctuaries, protecting 18,000 square miles of ocean. NOAA also manages 26 estuarine research reserves where studies on the land-sea interface are encouraged. The founding of sanctuaries and reserves reinforces the ethic that President Theodore Roosevelt expressed in regard to the national parks—an attitude that underlies protective laws and in ways transcends them: "The nation behaves well if it treats the natural resources as assets which it must turn over to the next generation increased, and not impaired, in value."

Bruce Babbitt, the U. S. Secretary of the Interior, in a 1994 NATIONAL GEO-GRAPHIC story honoring the National Park Service observed: "At the end of the last century...John Muir and Theodore Roosevelt foresaw the onslaught of urban settlers in the region and moved swiftly to protect lands that remain, even to this day, splendid and unique. The early conservationists set these lands aside as national parks—a simple idea...as...American as jazz and baseball." At the end of this century, pressures on the wild ocean from overfishing, waste disposal, and other polluting actions have inspired a sense of urgency about taking similar protective measures for the nation's ocean resources. Marine scientist Carl Safina observed in *Song for the Blue Ocean:* "Just as the land ethic grew into the conservation and environmental consciousness of the late 20th century, the sea ethic will logically expand our view of wildlife and its values throughout the oceans."

In this spirit, *Wild Ocean* explores the 12 national marine sanctuaries and reveals their natural and historic treasures. These special places circle the continent like a necklace, with two distant gems, one in Hawaii, the other in American Samoa. Two chapters in this volume reflect the profound impact temperature has on what kind of life can prosper where: In warm-water systems—the Florida Keys, the Flower Gardens in the

Gulf of Mexico, the Hawaiian Islands Humpback Whale Sanctuary, American Samoa, and Gray's Reef off the coast of Georgia—flourish reefs of coral, sponges, and a profusion of other life. Cool-water systems—at Stellwagen Bank in the Northeast, the Olympic Coast Sanctuary in the Northwest, and Cordell Bank, Gulf of the Farallones, Monterey, and the Channel Islands, all in California—give rise to distinctive assemblages of creatures. "The Mammalian Connection" focuses on marine mammals, including a few wide-ranging species that may turn up in all the sanctuaries. "A New Way of Looking at Fish" considers fish as wildlife whose living presence is as important to the health of oceans as wild birds are to terrestrial systems. "The Sweep of Time" traces the history of life itself in all the sanctuaries through to our own human history, from Atlantic waters where horseshoe crabs of ancient lineage swim, to shipwrecks, which serve as time capsules, such as the Civil War's U.S.S. *Monitor,* off the coast of North Carolina. Finally, "The Future" focuses on sanctuaries in the making—and how everyone can help support them. All represent an ethic of caring, an undersea version of the system of terrestrial national parks often said to be the "best idea America ever had."

Further, *Wild Ocean* will explore what the sanctuaries can mean to every person: To a diver in the Florida Keys gliding among the branches of one of the last healthy stands of elkhorn coral in the United States, a sanctuary is an insurance policy taken out by the nation to protect the future of the reefs. To a motel operator, it represents a national commitment to keep the ocean attractive for visitors who will sustain the area's economy. To schoolchildren, a sanctuary may be a playground with appealing creatures, reefs, and shores. To a scientist, it is a natural laboratory crammed with recipes for life developed over millions of years. To fishermen, sanctuaries may be the best hope they—and the fish—have for perpetuation of more fish. Vacationers might define any of the sanctuaries as "priceless national treasures."

In time, the definition of marine sanctuaries will reflect changing needs—and changing attitudes. Today, sanctuaries are not truly sacrosanct, but they are becoming recognized as a good idea, ecologically and economically. They are places in the sea as elusive as a sea breeze, as tangible as a singing whale. They are beautiful, or priceless, or rare bargains, or long-term assets, or fun, or all of these and more. Above all, they are now, and with care will continue to be, special. Each of us can have the pleasure of defining what that means.

Throughout this volume, thoughts by various caring people are highlighted apart from the narrative, to provide a kind of background music celebrating America's wild ocean. I join Wolcott Henry and the others represented here in conveying an underlying message of hope—that the places brought to you on these pages will be the foundation for an enduring ocean legacy, a gift from the 20th century to all who follow.

Long before knights in shining armor lived in castles on the land, jewel-like arrow crabs danced in bright-hued cathedrals…and they still do.

CHAPTER ONE

THE MAMMALIAN CONNECTION

The hollow echoed soundings of the deep,
Flutter and groan,
As heft and fluke of whales roll south.

Exhaled the song is sung—the circle closed,
The scale then mounts on rhythmic silver wings
And once again, the pod in chorus, blows
And in a moment's grace—creation sings.

MARGARET WENTWORTH OWING
VOICE FROM THE SEA

VOLUPTUOUS LIPS, smooth curves, alluring, undulating grace....
For a moment, I could almost imagine that the manatee I was watching was a matronly mermaid ambling over a lawn of seagrass in the
Florida Keys National Marine Sanctuary. For me, this was a rare
encounter, a chance to glimpse a one-ton creature whose relatives, dugongs and
sea cows, are thought to have inspired stories of mermaids among sailors. For
the manatee, my presence—a primate in her backyard—aroused only casual interest. She probably had seen many of my kind before, and as a dedicated plant-
eater, recognized me as neither edible nor, in these protected waters, formidable.

This plump "water baby" and other marine mammals—whales, dolphins, seals, sea lions, and sea otters—have inspired myths and legends
throughout their long history of interactions with us, and rightly so. The
behavior of sea mammals is often so hauntingly human. They play, nurse,
and care for their young, forge lasting bonds with one another, solve problems, sleep, eat, travel…and return home. Most seem to have a sense of place,
some remaining for most of their lives within a few miles of where they were
born; others range widely, over thousands of miles in one season. Many

Red mangroves border the shores of Biscayne Bay. In the nearby Florida Keys,
3,700 square miles of ocean have been designated as a national marine sanctuary,
where manatees and more than a dozen other marine mammals find refuge.

PRECEDING PAGES: *The parallel history of primates and marine mammals,*
one largely on the land, the other in the sea, has recently converged as we begin to meet
creatures, such as this manatee, in their aquatic realm, face to face.

marine mammals spend time feeding, breeding, or basking within one or more of the nation's marine sanctuaries, and for some, a sanctuary may be their primary home. Like cats, dogs, horses, and humans, each dolphin, whale, or seal is very much an individual, with special quirks and ways that set him or her apart from every other one of its kind.

In common with us and all other mammals and birds, sea mammals have four-chambered hearts that pump warm blood filled with dissolved oxygen that they obtain not from the sea, as fish do, but from the sky, inhaling air into lungs as we do. I try to imagine what it must be like to sleep suspended within—not on—the ultimate water bed, and even when dreaming to unfailingly respond to the insistent, frequent need to breathe.

We carry the sea with us.
We weep and sweat and bleed salt,
and if we go far enough back down our family tree to the trunk
we can understand why there is a feeling of kinship.
To me all life in the sea is family.

HUGH DOWNS
ABC NEWS 20/20

As I watched, the manatee surfaced, blowing a soft "whoosh" of warm breath from two wide nostrils set in a broad, marshmallow face more likely to inspire smiles than thoughts of a romantic interlude with a mermaid, unless, perhaps, the observer is a male manatee. Rounded fingernails—but no fingers—marked the tips of her flippers; fine bristles sprouted from her chubby chin, and her silver-gray shoulders hosted a fetching gloss of green algae. This blimplike beauty was one of about 2,500 of her kind in the United States—a rare creature indeed compared to the many millions of people who share the same region of the planet.

Like so many creatures, her kind has been a source of easy meals for people who have encountered them over the ages. One large relative, the Steller's sea cow, the sole species of a distinctive family discovered in the Bering Sea in 1741, was entirely eradicated within 27 years—a victim of its own docile good nature and good taste. For millennia, sea creatures were protected primarily by their inaccessibility, but no longer. Today the 9 species of great whales and the more than 50 kinds of "small" dolphins, whales, and porpoises, as well as other marine mammals have been reduced to frighteningly low levels as high-tech methods have been applied to finding and taking ocean wildlife.

No longer hunted in North America for food, manatees nonetheless are considered highly endangered because their numbers are low, reproduction is slow, and mortality from pollution and collisions with fast boats is high. In recent years, the death of hundreds has been linked to red tides of increasing size and toxicity in Florida waters. Protection for the shallow coastal waters they require for feeding, breeding, and everyday living is absolutely essential for their survival—but it puts them in direct conflict with growing numbers of people who are attracted to the same places.

While manatee survival was not the primary reason for naming 3,700 square miles of ocean surrounding the Florida Keys as a marine sanctuary in 1990, that action provides a lifeline for them and for the entire ecosystem of which they—and we—are a part. The broad, shallow beds of sea grasses and benthic algae are the manatee's pastures, but those same undersea fields are nurseries for fish, shrimp, and hosts of other organisms that are essential components of a productive marine system. The plants also churn enormous quantities of oxygen into the surrounding sea and the atmosphere above, replenishing the fragile envelope of air that makes Earth a hospitable place for man and manatee. One thing is sure: For many people, manatees have become an engaging symbol of why we should take care of the ocean. Stuffed manatee toys and bumper stickers, cards, books, billboards, and T-shirts celebrate recognition by people that manatees matter.

If sea creatures could designate ambassadors to engage humankind, to cause us to care about the ocean, to lure us there to see for ourselves the joy of being aquatic on a planet dominated by water, dolphins would be an excellent choice. Even without the formalities of state, dolphins have inspired a passionate sense of caring in people worldwide, throughout history.

What is it about dolphins that inspires affection? Horace Dobbs, a dedicated expert on dolphins, believes they have many aspects of the human character that we like to find in our friends, and they "seem to lack the traits that we find objectionable...." He cites their intelligence, curiosity, empathy, and lack of aggression toward us, although they are fully capable of killing sharks and other creatures as large as they. They appear to have an innate sense of fun;

FOLLOWING PAGES: *Atlantic spotted dolphins form moving cities with fluid boundaries. For them, as for most other marine mammals, sound is as important as sight is to us for sensing their surroundings and communicating with one another.*

If sea creatures could appoint ambassadors,
they might choose dolphins to forge bonds of understanding between
humankind and themselves, a fanciful idea made real by
the bottlenosed porpoise shown above.
Spinner dolphins, such as the one leaping at left, are among the many
creatures benefiting from research and education programs in
the Hawaiian Islands Humpback Whale
National Marine Sanctuary.

some deliberately release air in such a way as to create an undersea version of smoke rings—perfect circles exhaled from the dolphin's blowhole. They play among themselves and, under the right circumstances, involve us in the action, as actor Robin Williams discovered while swimming with dolphins off the coast of Florida: "I was observed and acoustically scanned by a being whose intensity and curiosity matched mine. We spent 45 minutes together...and at the end...he definitely knew more about me than I knew about him. If knowledge is intelligence, I was swimming in the shallow end of the gene pool."

As a scientist and mother swimming with my three young children and a wild dolphin, *Stenella longirostris,* I witnessed such behavior. Usually dolphins live in large social groups. This one was a loner who for weeks had shown friendly interest in the only other mammals in the area—snorkelers, divers, and an occasional dog swimming near a local beach resort.

Imitating the sleek creature's movements my son, Richie, held his flippered feet closely together and undulated his whole body, an action that sent the dolphin into spirals of apparent delight. My eldest, Elizabeth, attracted his interest with her long, shining mane of red-gold hair. The dolphin approached, peppering her with the rapid staccato sounds of echolocation and a series of high "weeeps!" Coming closer, he gently mouthed locks of her hair, then carefully allowed silken strands to flow through his teeth, as if trying to determine their nature. Then with alarm, I watched my youngest, Gale, reach out and loop her small fingers around the dolphin's dorsal fin. She had been instructed to let the dolphin make all the overtures, but her gesture was as natural as touching hands with a new friend.

I have had the joy of a close encounter of the aquatic kind.
I was observed and acoustically scanned by a being whose intensity and curiosity
matched mine. Like me he was a middle-aged male,
albeit of the spotted dolphin variety.

ROBIN WILLIAMS
ACTOR AND COMEDIAN

Although there is a long history of contacts among people, dolphins, and other mammals of the sea, our respective paths of adaptation—on land and in water—have left us with much to learn about each other: Humans have fine-tuned bipedal locomotion, but only in the past century have we developed tools that extend our senses—and our range—into the deepest parts of the sea, and aloft—far beyond the edge of Earth's atmosphere.

It is one of the quests of the Sustainable Seas Expeditions (see Introduction) to descend to and explore places previously inaccessible to us. For this, researchers in all the sanctuaries will use newly developed, one-person submersibles called *DeepWorker 2000*. These can descend to 2000 feet.

Without technological advances, but with fine minds, dolphins and whales form societies, travel unerringly with no maps or obvious highways, survive storms without special shelters, find food, raise their young, communicate with intricate, hauntingly beautiful sounds, and generally thrive in the medium that even today remains largely unknown, inhospitable, and inaccessible to most air-breathing creatures, including humans.

Biologists Karen Pryor and Kenneth Norris recently assembled a report on dolphins that provides exciting new insights into what we know—and more important, don't know. Not surprisingly, truth proves more wondrous than even the best of sea stories. We now know that social structures vary dramatically, from killer whales, who tend to live in durable, small, close-knit societies, to spinner dolphins, who move in large, fluctuating groups like mobile, seagoing cities, with fluid boundaries populated by changing families within. Recently, discoveries have been made about dusky dolphins, whose social structure shifts with the choice of prey; about spotted dolphins, who live in male-dominated groups; and about pilot whales, who travel in clusters without adult males but with very old "grandmothers." These elders' role may be linked to reliance on their valued experience in finding food, caring for young, and other knowledge.

Yet even in the coastal waters of the United States, as the habits of marine mammals are just beginning to come into focus, there are coincident alarming trends of decline for many once common species. Other creatures and entire ecosystems are in trouble, too, but our empathy for dolphins and whales links us to the sea in ways not as easily bridged by concerns over declining populations of clams, cod, urchins, or squid.

In 1972, the U.S. Marine Mammal Protection Act was initiated in part by growing concern for dolphins being caught in the nets of tuna fishermen. While people were willing to have wild fish taken for market, there was great resistance to the sacrifice of dolphins as "by-catch," and growing support for protection of all marine mammals. In addition, the act made it unlawful to harm marine mammals in U.S. waters, with a few exceptions.

Although curbing the killing is foremost in helping declining species recover, it isn't enough. Like people, most creatures require reliable sources of food, clean water, and suitable places for their young to grow up, in short—a hospitable environment. Within the act was unprecedented recognition that habitat protection "to maintain the health and stability of the marine ecosystem...was vital to the protection of the species involved." That same year came the legislation authorizing National Marine Sanctuaries.

In sanctuaries, not single animals, but entire ecosystems, are protected. And with good reason: Saving blue whales, for instance, but capturing the krill they require for sustenance, is simply shifting death by harpoon to death from starvation. Prohibiting the killing of seals but displacing them from beaches needed for raising their young ends their future. Marine sanctuaries provide safe havens, small but vital insurance policies against such disasters.

Russell DeConti of the Center for Coastal Studies has considered the difficulties in establishing marine sanctuaries: "Protecting an environment of such dynamic and transient qualities presents special challenges...there are no obvious borders or points of entry and no physical barriers.... The sanctuary is never the same, with its boundaries fixed mainly in our minds and an ocean, quite literally, flowing through them." This is particularly true for whales, whose migration routes pass through many sanctuaries.

What is a marine sanctuary.
When you look underneath, you discover a world which is truly
a national treasure and worthy of protection
for generations to come.

ALLEN TOM
SUPERINTENDENT, HAWAIIAN ISLANDS HUMPBACK WHALE MARINE SANCTUARY

Biologist Peter Tyack observes, "Habitat requirements for whales are like the complex system required for modern aviation. Jets are free to cover most of the globe. While they seem free from Earth, they require specialized communication and navigation gear on the ground as well as ground services such as landing strips and fuel supplies."

Such factors were very much on the balance sheet when a sanctuary for the notorious "singing whales," the humpbacks, was proposed for the Hawaiian Islands. I first heard about the idea when I went to the island of Maui in 1977 to embark on a study of the species Herman Melville described as "the most gamesome and light-hearted of all the whales." That year, whale song experts Roger Payne, Katherine Payne, and *(continued on page 38)*

As distinctive as a fingerprint, a humpback whale's one-of-a-kind tail
pattern identifies it. Since the 1970s researchers have cataloged hundreds of individual
humpbacks on both coasts of the United States, as well as in Hawaii and Alaska.

FOLLOWING PAGES: *As curious about us as we are about them, humpbacks
often give new meaning to the term "whale-watching."*

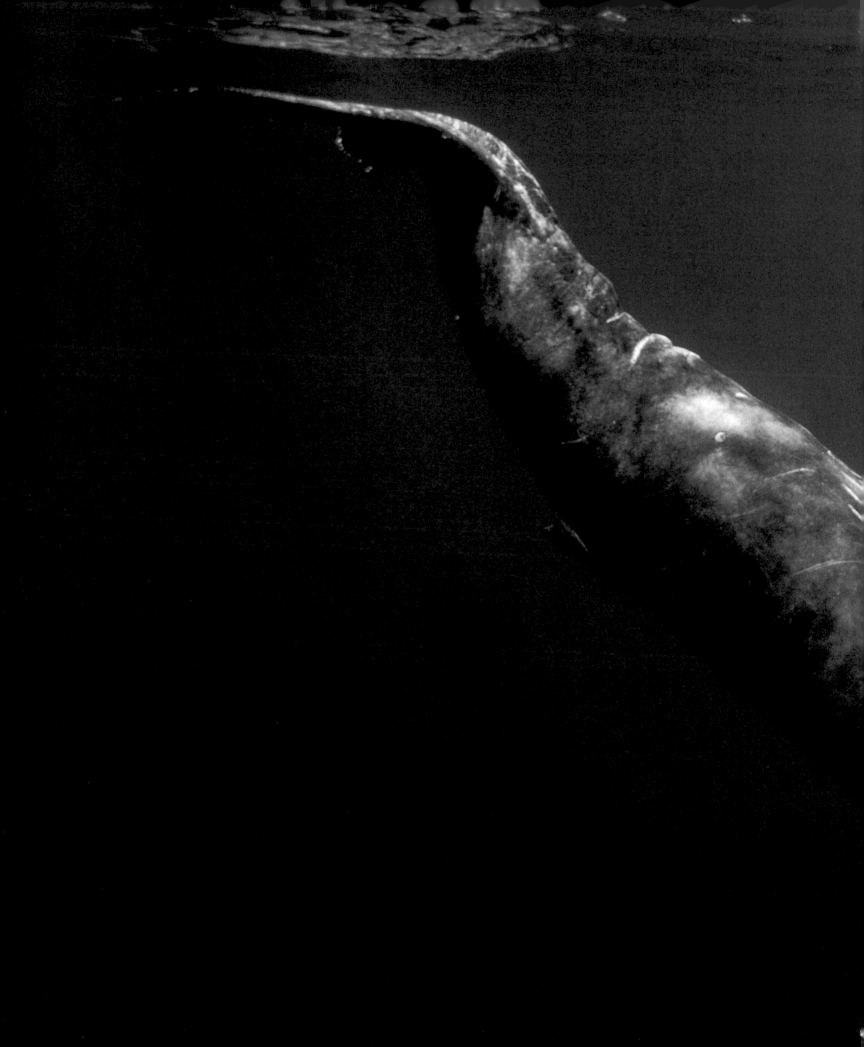

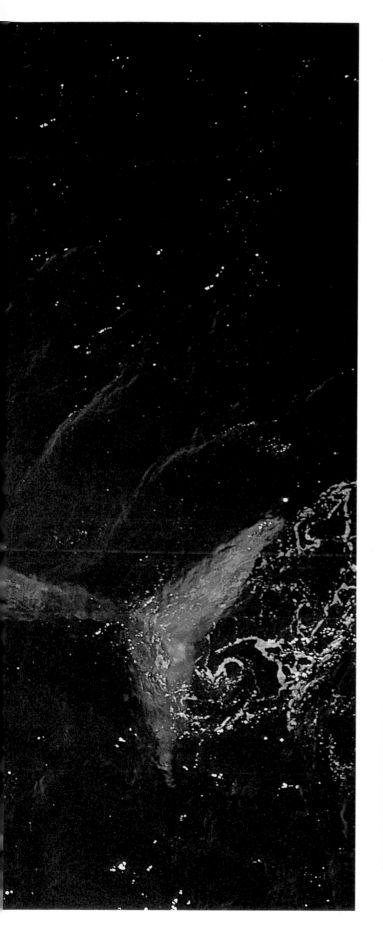

Beautiful creatures in their own right,
billions of inch-long, dark-eyed krill,
like the one above, provide fuel for
blue whales, Earth's largest creatures. Below,
a blue whale gets a mouthful of krill.
Bill Douros, superintendent of the
Monterey Bay National Marine Sanctuary,
has often seen ocean giants such as the one
at left cruising the California coast.
He says, "Once, I spent an hour with a
blue whale off Monterey, watching it
breathe. It changed my life."

Sperm whales, creatures with
the largest brains ever, have complex,
close-knit societies. They can
hold their breath for an hour and dive
more than a mile deep in search
of their favorite food—squid.
Hal Whitehead, who has spent years
studying these mysterious animals,
describes an underwater encounter
in Voyage to the Whales:
"There is the jaw, straight, firm,
and lined with white.... Above stretches
the forehead, its 'lofty purpose'
undisclosed, a symbol of all that the
whale keeps hidden. Behind are
the flippers that steer, that touch.
Closest is the eye. Timid and
curious, it watches me."

Peter Tyack planned to join forces with me and underwater photographers Al Giddings and Chuck Nicklin, to try to correlate the mysterious and achingly beautiful sounds of the whales with their behavior underwater. My personal dream was to emulate Jane Goodall's approach to learning about chimpanzees—to be with the whales on their own terms, and get to know individuals over many months and years. Then came the reality.

Awash in a vast, open-ocean Jacuzzi—the wake of a diving whale—I surfaced for air two miles offshore from Lahaina, Hawaii's popular coastal resort, within what is now the sanctuary that boasts the longest name: Hawaiian Islands Humpback Whale National Marine Sanctuary. Below, five humpbacks arched through blue water, each about 40 feet long and, from the tips of their 15-foot-long flippers and across their broad backs, about 40 feet wide. I must have appeared to them as a mouse might to me—cute, but hardly worth considering. Yet one of the huge creatures swept away from the others and, with gigantic grace, glided straight for me. It was a hauntingly human gesture—a childlike, scientist-like expression of curiosity.

I had come to Hawaii to study whales; it was disconcerting to be the subject of observations myself. In a moment, the great animal was an arm's length away, one flipper arched to avoid collision, her huge eyes moving slightly as she passed. Within that great body beat a heart like my own on a colossal scale, pumping warm blood through a warm body, muscles rippling from attachments connected to a long, strong backbone. Two fellow mammals, each the product of millions of years of history on the same planet, one largely terrestrial, the other essentially aquatic, regarded each other, each wondering, perhaps, what the other might do next.

I don't know about the whale, but for me the experience was life changing. Since then, I have read new meaning into the words of Aldo Leopold, who wrote in *A Sand County Almanac:* "We know now what was unknown to all the preceding caravan of generations, that men are only fellow voyagers with other creatures.... This new knowledge should have given us, by this time, a sense of kinship...a wish to live and let live; a sense of wonder over the magnitude and duration of the biotic enterprise."

Recalling visions of those first encounters with whales, I can and do easily enliven boring meetings, long waits at checkout counters, and the monotony of traffic jams—such as the one I was once trapped in on my way from Cape Cod to Boston. Suddenly my daydreaming took shape. Dead ahead I could see whales, not drifting across my mind's eye, but right there in front of me! I laughed out loud, realizing then that what I beheld was a giant painting splashed across the Summerfield Building, some 10 stories high, 125 feet wide, arising like a dream amid gray buildings and traffic. Wyland, a dashing young artist with a flying brush, had produced one of his distinctive murals, driven by his vision that "yet unborn children will be able to see a great whale swimming free...."

Like Wyland, hundreds of artists, poets, writers, and perhaps most promising of all, thousands of schoolchildren, have been motivated to capture the spirit of whales and dolphins in sculptures, paintings, songs, and stories. But the Boston whale was more portrait than essence of whale. It was a particular, special whale, well-known to many as "Salt," because of a distinctive patch of white near her dorsal fin. Along with Al Avellar, an astute fisherman from Provincetown, Massachusetts, Salt helped inspire the multi-million-dollar industry in New England known as whale-watching. Protecting marine creatures from harm because we care about them for their own sakes provides powerful incentive to develop appropriate policies and establish sanctuaries where whales are safe. But having economic incentives helps, too. A dead whale can be sold once for a finite number of pounds of meat and so many barrels of oil. Salt, alive, has helped generate sustained prosperity for local communities who host paying customers who come to see her and her pals year after year. First sighted and named in 1976, she has given birth to seven calves since 1980, and in 1992 became a grandmother.

Large numbers of whales, cod, and tuna have been seeking the sanctuary of
Stellwagen Bank since New Englanders began to record such things.
It took us until 1992 to formally recognize [it]....
With the sanctuary in place, the future looks bright, but perhaps
we should have responded sooner to what
these animals were telling us.

BRAD BARR
SANCTUARY MANAGER, STELLWAGEN BANK MARINE SANCTUARY

Avellar toyed with the idea of conducting whale-watching trips in 1959 while taking people fishing. "They dropped the poles," he said, "when whales came around. I figured if fishermen would look, there must be something to whale-watching." At first, "people wouldn't pay a nickel to go look for whales." But in the early 1970s attitudes began to change. Some regard the new busi-

WHALE TALES

*Gray whales' breeding and feeding areas are thousands of miles apart. At left,
a California gray whale cruises a kelp forest in northern California in one part of its
range; another, above, delights whale-watchers in a nursery area in Baja California.*

ONCE CALLED "devilfish" by whalers for their ferocious response to being harpooned, gray whales are now largely protected worldwide. Our change of attitude and 50 years of protective measures have been rewarded with recovery of these whales from near-extinction to a population of more than 20,000—and a new relationship. Now called "the friendlies" for their gentle, curious behavior toward people in small boats, gray whales are among the dozens of marine mammals that benefit from the National Marine Sanctuary Program. For wide-ranging species, including most whales, international cooperation is vital. For gray whales, the U. S. is responsible for much of the range where feeding occurs. The sanctuaries afford the chance to observe their habits as bottom feeders. Jim Darling notes in his *Wild Whales:* "They lie on their sides and suck in mouthfuls of the bottom. Then they squirt the sand ...through baleen filters." Breeding and calving largely occur in a few protected warm-water lagoons along the coast of Baja California.

ness now generating hundreds of millions of dollars annually as a heaven-sent alternative to sharply declining revenues from commercial fishing. But Avellar says, "There are no miracles to whale-watching; the miracles are the whales and the folks' enthusiasm for them."

Many now sign up for whale-watching trips to the Channel Islands, Monterey Bay, and the waters near San Francisco, in the hope that they will be able to meet the largest animal ever to occupy Earth—the great blue whale. For blue whales, superlatives seem superfluous. Put simply, they may attain one hundred feet in length, live to be one hundred years old, and require hundreds of tons of food every year to power them over the hundreds of thousands of square miles of their oceanic range. On land, a giant Mesozoic dinosaur, *Brachiosaurus,* is renowned because it is believed to have weighed as much as 80 tons. But a blue whale weighs more than a ton a foot; a 50-ton whale may not yet have reached puberty.

What must it be like to be the largest creature, ever—to be so large that other whales seem like minnows, and all of the ocean about the size of a swimming pool? Whale scientist Roger Payne imagines that "As the largest animal…you could afford to be gentle, to view life without fear, to play in the dark, to sleep soundly anywhere, whenever and wherever and however you liked, and to greet the world in peace." Roger adds, "It is this sense of tranquility—of life without urgency, power without aggression—that has won my heart to whales."

In one of nature's wonderful ironies, these largest of all creatures fuel their energy needs by consuming some of the smallest: tons of tiny krill, shrimplike crustaceans that in turn munch on massive quantities of miniscule plants. Like other plankton-feeding whales, blues snare their small prey using bristly strands of baleen that take the place of teeth in the whale's upper jaw. Many of the largest land animals eat low on the food chain, too, notably elephants, hippopotamuses, gorillas, pandas, wildebeests, buffaloes, horses, and caribou. These herbivores are one step removed from tapping directly into the sun's energy, which is fixed by plants through the magic of photosynthesis. Baleen whales are at least two steps away when krill are on their menu. A terrestrial equivalent for a krill-eating whale would be a gigantic version of a moose powered by a diet of gnats.

Despite their great size, whales can quickly lose sight of one another at night or in murky water. Sound—delivering it and receiving it—is the primary mode of communication among cetaceans of all sorts, from the booming low-frequency groans uttered by blue, sei, bowhead, humpback, and other baleen whales that may travel and be received by other whales across hundreds or even thousands of miles of ocean, to piercing, high-pitched squeals and rapid clicks emitted by toothed whales, including dolphins and pilot and sperm whales. It seems reasonable to suppose that cetaceans can and do convey various kinds of information to one another, although it would help to be a whale to really understand the nature of the messages.

One person who has come close to thinking like a whale is Ken Norris. He has studied the function of the rounded heads of various toothed cetaceans that feature an oil-filled structure, or "melon," which focuses emitted sounds. He thinks that the largest toothed whales, the cachalots, or sperm whales, have developed special refinements that may allow them to stun or confuse their prey with bursts of intense, focused sound.

Once among the most sought-after prey themselves by whalers, sperm whales today are protected worldwide through agreements signed by more than 40 countries. These whales are as cosmopolitan in the sea as we are on the land, ranging throughout all the wild ocean except the coldest areas of the Arctic and Antarctic. So how, you might ask, can the protection of a few scattered areas in the vastness of the ocean serve to protect creatures such as these—or any wide-ranging species, for that matter?

Policies such as the U.S. Marine Mammal Protection Act afford blanket immunity from killing—with a few notable exceptions. Another is the International Whaling Commission's overall moratorium, in 1980, on the taking of great whales worldwide—with other notable exceptions. Within these broad efforts to ensure continuity for marine mammals, there is a vital role for marine sanctuaries, not the least being that they are places where people can encounter these creatures, and in so doing, begin to understand their needs: that what they require is fundamentally what we require. Laws help, of course, but they may be less important if an underlying ethic of caring is in place; without such an ethic, laws are rarely enforceable.

No creature better illustrates the changing ethic about our relationship with sea creatures generally, and with the sea itself, than the California gray whale, a medium-to-large-size great whale about whom we demonstrate curious and continuing ambivalence. Hunted to near extinction by the early part of the 20th century as a source of oil, meat, and bone, grays were widely regarded as a dangerous "devilfish"—and no wonder. The famous whaler Capt. Charles Melville Scammon recorded in 1858 the hazards in store for those who harpooned baby whales to draw their mothers close enough to kill: "Hardly a day passes but there is an upsetting or staving of boats, the crews receiving bruises, cuts, and in many instances, having limbs broken...."

Today gray whales have a new name—"the friendlies." Protected since 1937 by international agreements, they have increased in number and now recognize humans as benign onlookers rather than dangerous enemies. The Mexican government established several quiet, shallow nursery lagoons along Baja California as sanctuaries for the whales, and all along the thousands of miles of western coastline of North America, migrating whales could enjoy safety from commercial hunters as they traveled between vital feeding areas.

I first visited one of the nurseries in 1979, soon after news that "curious whales" were approaching small boats and allowing their great noses to be patted. With my young daughter, one hundredth of a whale's size, I glided in a rubber boat one third the length of a gray whale. Suddenly, amid a swirl of water, something dark lifted out of the sea—an absurd-looking face, encrusted with barnacles. I barely registered the image before it withdrew—and reappeared, a great, glistening eye regarding us from a new angle a mere 20 yards away! I had hoped to engage in a bit of whale-watching, but here was a whale…watching.

Recently recognizing the amazing recovery of gray whales from near extinction to a healthy population of more than 20,000, the International Whaling Commission (IWC) granted permission to kill a small number of gray whales to Makah tribesmen who live in a coastal nation adjacent to the Olympic Coast National Marine Sanctuary. The Makah make a case for taking whales as vital to their cultural heritage: The quality of their lives, if not their livelihoods, is at stake. Troubling to some is that the same individual whales acclimated to the benign touch of humans throughout most of their range may be greeted with harpoons when they swim within the 3,310 square miles designated as the Olympic Coast Sanctuary, and nearby waters.

Conflicts also arise about the fate of seals, sea lions, and sea otters. For years valued mostly as a source of food and oil, or for their soft, warm pelts, all these marine mammals presently are viewed by some as competitors with fishermen for dwindling populations of fish and shellfish.

It is easy to feel empathy for creatures who individually or in playful camaraderie surf waves like champions, gliding along a wave crest for a long, sweeping ride, and ducking out just before crashing. Like exuberant puppies, sea lions sometimes surround scuba divers, tugging at swim fins, capturing exhaled bubbles, and generally romping around with speed and grace that combine the best athletic attributes of acrobats, eels, and ballerinas.

These appealing creatures had already been drastically decimated by human hunters before the beginning of the 20th century. Northern elephant seals, now a frequent sight in the Monterey Bay and Channel Islands National Marine Sanctuaries, were once reduced to less than 100 individuals—largely because of their valuable oil-rich blubber.

It is a wonder that their doglike cousins, the harbor seals, have survived to see the 21st century at all. Not only captured as a source of food and fur, they have also been targeted for elimination as pests. From 1888 to as recently as 1962, Massachusetts offered a bounty on harbor seals to reduce their population and increase the number of fish caught by fishermen. Presently, harbor seals have made a strong comeback in the Northeast, although they are still uncommon elsewhere along the eastern seaboard. They are among the marine mammals that bring joy to visitors at the Stellwagen Bank National Marine Sanctuary, at the mouth of Massachusetts Bay. Their western counterpart, a different species with similar habits, though protected for many years, are low in numbers. When viewed as a commodity or competitor, it seems difficult to focus on a creatures' appealing characteristics—their playfulness and caring for their young, their vital but less obvious contributions to perpetuating the good health of wild ocean systems that yield benefits back to them—and to us.

And yet, Wallace Stegner's thoughts about California mountain lions might apply equally to sea lions, seals, and other marine mammals sometimes sized up as nuisances: "Controls we may need, what is called game-management we may need, for we have engrossed the Earth and must now play God to the other species. But deliberate war on any species, especially a species of such evolved beauty and precise function, diminishes, endangers, and brutalizes us. If we cannot live in harmony with other forms of life, if we cannot control our hostility toward the Earth and its creatures, how shall we ever learn to control our hostility toward each other?"

Perhaps through the eyes of dolphins, of whales, of a newly born sea lion pup, or even our own children, we will see ourselves more clearly and find answers that will serve us well as the next phase of our shared existence on a largely aquatic planet unfolds.

FOLLOWING PAGES: *Northern fur seals and California sea lions share the beach on Point Bennett at San Miguel Island of Channel Islands National Park. Some 1,658 square miles of protected ocean— the Channel Islands National Marine Sanctuary—borders the park.*

Jim Fowler of television's Wild Kingdom *recalls his first dive with a sea lion, like the one at left, in the Channel Islands Marine Sanctuary. "I met a playful pup face to face in the kelp forest. The swaying rhythm of the kelp and the mysterious blue darkness into which all objects disappear made me feel humble, yet curiously at home." A dominant male northern elephant seal, above, declares his seniority; below, a youngster behaves like any kid at the beach. Protected within park boundaries through the 1972 Marine Mammal Protection Act, elephant seals, once hunted for their blubber, are making a comeback.*

Taking the plunge,
a California sea lion bridges the
gap between its two worlds.
Superbly adapted for moving
in the sea, where it finds food and fun,
the agile mammal also remains
linked to the land for resting and
warming up between swims,
for socializing, and for giving birth to
its pups. In the Channel Islands
two agencies monitor this dual realm:
for the land, the National Park
Service, and for the sea, the National
Marine Sanctuary Program.

CHAPTER TWO

IN WARM
WATERS

I hate to be making platitudes
But I like warmer latitudes.

ARCH E. BENTHIC
THE ID OF THE SQUID

———————————————

WHERE THE SHORELINE meets the sea begins a vast, unexplored part of the country with high mountains, steep canyons, mighty rivers, broad plains, mysterious caves, dense forests—all crowded with extraordinary wildlife, including creatures most people have never seen, even in photographs. Twenty thousand years ago and even as recently as ten thousand years ago, much of that varied terrain marked the edge of the present United States; now it is submerged. So much of Earth's water was locked up in continental ice sheets at the height of the last ice age that sea level, worldwide, was as much as 300 feet below where it is now. Today, 17 miles east of Sapelo Island, offshore from Savannah, Georgia, and 60 feet down, a hidden ancient coastline gives rise to a modern miracle: a luxuriant reef, glowing with light and life—a thriving warm-water system.

Ocean temperature at the surface is largely determined by latitude and season, with more heat received from the sun at the Equator than at higher or lower latitudes. Currents, some warm, some cold, driven by winds, density differentials, and the Earth's motion flow like rivers through the surrounding sea, dramatically altering the nature of weather and climate locally—and globally.

If not for the mellowing influence of the Gulf Stream's tropical push far into the North Atlantic, much of the northeastern United States and northern Europe would stay frozen most of the year, and Gray's Reef probably would

*Millions of people are drawn every year to the jewel-clear waters
of the Florida Keys National Marine Sanctuary. The swath of blue ocean
surrounds an arc of islands that sweeps more than a hundred miles
to the south and west from Miami.*

PRECEDING PAGES: *An improbable richness of life adorns
ancient shorelines at Gray's Reef Marine Sanctuary, 17 miles offshore
from Sapelo Island, Georgia—and 60 feet down.*

harbor creatures normally at home in the far north.

Long before I had a chance to dive along the Georgia coast, I had heard about Gray's Reef, a place well known to local fishermen and acknowledged by numerous fish, turtles, and the rare northern right whales as an attractive undersea oasis rising from a generally level seafloor, the right place to find food and shelter or to meet others of their kind. Now one of the nation's marine sanctuaries, the reef typically is awash in water clear enough so that from the surface you can make out in the depths below the broad dark outlines of sponges and great, bushy bryozoans.

Influenced by the northbound Gulf Stream, coastal Georgia attracts tropical fish and other warm-water creatures, but does not maintain the sustained range of temperature favored by reef-building corals—18° to 30° Celsius. On my first visit there, an undersea fog of fine sediment and rich plankton had moved in. Yet, what came into focus as I neared bottom resembled places known and loved by millions of visitors throughout the Florida Keys and the Caribbean: sponges, bright clumps of algae, slender fingers of soft coral, some nameless yellow lumps, and a shimmer of small fish—a kaleidoscope of shapes and colors. I glanced up in time to catch six pairs of eyes staring at me through a green haze: six sleek, swift, obviously curious amberjack, checking me out.

In times past, Gray's Reef and much of the rest of the northern hemisphere have been much colder—and at other times, significantly more tropical, as ice ages have come and gone, creating the background regime of temperature that has much to do with what kinds of life occur where. In North America, as E. C. Pielou points out in *After the Ice Age,* "a little less than 20,000 years ago, the ice…covered all of Canada and the northern tier of the United States." The success of humankind has largely been a matter of being able to adapt to cold places by making clothing, building shelters, or harnessing fire or other energies, to keep us warm, or, when it's hot, to cool us off. Other creatures must make do with their innate ability to grow or shed layers of fat or fur, or shut down in some form of dormancy or hibernation in inclement weather, or migrate as temperatures change beyond their favored range. Others adapt through selection pressures to new thermal patterns, or they perish.

As I glided over Georgia's hidden gardens, I tried to imagine what it must have been like at the end of the last ice age, before the sea level began to rise, engulfing the coniferous forests and broad marshes that grew where I now swam. Bones of saber-toothed tigers, mastodons, and other large Pleistocene mammals have been recovered from the reef, and core samples drilled deep into the surrounding sediment give clues about what the area was like long ago. Gray's

Reef may have been an outer barrier island populated by Paleo-Indian communities who were drawn to the shore then just as we are today. More than half the world's population now lives within about 50 miles of the sea for reasons that probably haven't changed much in 20,000 years.

More than 200 years ago, before Meriwether Lewis and William Clark made their historic discoveries about the American West, an intrepid naturalist and poet, William Bartram, visited coastal Georgia and discovered on an offshore island bits of pottery from a culture that had lived there long ago. He found in a "mound of sea shell…fragments of earthern vessels, and other utensils, the manufacture of the ancients…. One pot…almost whole…was curiously wrought all over on the outside, representing basket work…."

Reed Bohne, manager of what is now the 23-square-mile Gray's Reef National Marine Sanctuary, which includes the area Bartram saw, says, "Bartram's wonderment at the magnificence of the virginlike territory of colonial America echoes across the centuries to us as we venture into our own new world beneath the waves…. His spirit shades our contemporary explorations." Today, Bohne says, "like the colonial traveler in the New World, we only now have the rudimentary tools to explore the undersea continents and fully marvel at the discoveries before us. Out yonder, down under, in the ocean we can still be the first person ever to set eyes on a particular reef, patch of kelp forest, or submarine volcano belching out a black mineral soup."

Designation of Gray's Reef as a national marine sanctuary happened largely because of the singleminded determination of one woman who never got to see the resident amberjack and angelfish face to face, and was not aware at the time of the reef's exciting archaeological and paleontological potential. But in the late 1970s, Jane Yarn, Georgia's "charming champion of coastal conservation" could and did recognize its recreational and biological significance. Of Yarn, President Jimmy Carter has said, "Without her insight and sensitivity, I could never have accomplished what I did environmentally. Her calm, patient leadership long since qualified Jane Yarn as a hero of mine."

He was her hero, too, a man who set the pace for the environment in ways not seen since the time of President Theodore Roosevelt. Four marine sanctuaries came into being as a consequence of actions taken during the Carter era: In addition to Gray's Reef, there were the Gulf of the Farallones and the Channel Islands in California, and in Florida, Looe Key, which subsequently merged with the much larger Florida Keys National Marine Sanctuary.

Carter remarked in 1999, "Some of my most gratifying achievements in public life relate to conservation. I think about the *(continued on page 62)*

"The best way to observe fish is to become a fish," wrote diving pioneer Jacques Cousteau in an October 1952 issue of NATIONAL GEOGRAPHIC. Since then, millions of people have slipped through the magical air-sea interface with scuba, snuba, or snorkeling gear, such as the divers use here, to explore coral reefs in the Florida Keys. Diving, according to photographer Norbert Wu, "is like being in a big, air-conditioned jungle [that's] cool, comfortable, filled with life, and [with] no mosquitoes...you glide with weightless ease.... It's the closest thing to flying."

FOLLOWING PAGES: Black-masked and flashing yellow, raccoon butterflyfish flow like liquid sunshine over a Hawaiian reef. These brilliant beauties are among the thousands of small, medium, and occasionally very large residents of the Hawaiian Islands Humpback Whale Marine Sanctuary.

landmark Alaska lands legislation near the end of my Presidency, in which we added over 150 million acres to the National Park and Wildlife Refuge Systems. I also think of the increase from two to six during those years of the protected marine sanctuaries off the coasts of the United States.... The world's oceans are critically threatened by overfishing, pollution, disease, and encroaching humanity. These vital protected pockets along the U.S. coasts must be preserved...."

The concerns voiced by Carter in 1999 are much the same as those articulated in 1929 by John Kunkel Small, eminent botanist, explorer, and author of a slim book, *From Eden to Sahara: Florida's Tragedy.* He wrote: "Here is a unique…tongue of land, extending hundreds of miles…almost to the Tropic of Cancer, where…subtropic and tropic regions not only meet, but mingle." With wistful eloquence, Small described the natural wonders, abundant prehistoric sites—and the "reckless, furious, even mad desire to destroy everything natural," beginning early in the 1800s. By Small's time, plume hunters had already come and gone, shattering the structure of ancient communities of egrets, spoonbills, ibis, and others. Otters and manatees had become rare, alligators scarce, and other creatures virtually nonexistent. Once he happened onto a small island, Long Pine Key, where in a rocky glen a carpet of rare fern grew "so luxuriantly that deer would lie in the dense beds and several times…arose…only feet in front of us." Returning later he "found houses…everywhere, but not a leaf of the fern!"

These vital protected pockets along U.S. coasts must be preserved and studied
as we learn to sustain the lifeblood of the blue planet.

JIMMY CARTER
FORMER U.S. PRESIDENT

Worried, Small urged that "this natural history…should be preserved, not only for its beauty, but also for its educational values…. It is not yet too late to act." The fading Eden he described on the land has nearly disappeared. Yet in the 1950s, many years after Small's warnings, I thought I had found a heaven on Earth when I first saw the Florida Keys: air-clear water, a profusion of fish, lobsters sauntering across shallow seagrass beds, mangrove tangles crowding marshy shores, large pink conchs plowing furrows through white sand. I did not then own flippers or a snorkel let alone have access to submersibles such as scientists will use during the Sustainable Seas Expeditions. I used only a face mask, a window on a splendid realm that even Small had not witnessed. I am certain much had changed since the 1920s, and changes still, but the Florida

Keys underwater was—and is—a paradise well worth enjoying—and saving.

Astronaut Mike Collins, who piloted the Apollo spacecraft around the moon while the first footprints were being planted there, is a nearby resident who favors protective measures in the Keys: "When we astronauts went to the moon, we pretty much knew what life-forms to expect—none! How different it is here in the Florida Keys Sanctuary…the astounding fecundity of this nursery makes it virtually certain that I will see something new and beautiful each time I visit."

When a series of events coincided in the late 1980s—dying coral reefs, concerns about pollution, and most dramatically, the grounding in 1989 of several large ships on reefs near popular diving and fishing areas in the Keys, Congress acted to formally designate 3,700 square miles of ocean around the Florida Keys as a national marine sanctuary.

Today millions of visitors to the Florida Keys swim, snorkel, snuba, scuba, or play along the shore. Some come to match wits with the fish and spend money on fishing gear and boats. Others, like bird- and whale-watchers, are captivated by a new and inspired way of looking at fish alive.

Not long ago, Fred Rogers, genial television hero to the under-six crowd and their parents, filmed a segment in the Florida Keys for his popular show, *Mr. Rogers' Neighborhood.* A queen angelfish seemed to take a liking to him, as fish sometimes do with a swimmer who moves as effortlessly as Rogers; she deliberately circled around and peered into his face mask, meeting his eyes, then trailed along after him as he made his way over a small forest of pale sea fans and rounded lumps of brain coral. Translucent, lavender moon jellies pulsed by, and a shower of silver minnows parted as one when he swam into their midst. After filming, the crew assembled for dinner at a local restaurant, and nearly everyone ordered seafood. But not Rogers. In his quiet, steady voice he said, "I can't imagine eating fish after what we saw today." Like songbirds, fish offer to some values that transcend the gastronomic.

"It did not occur to me that fish can be recognized as individuals," one of Rogers' crew confided. That day in the Keys Sanctuary had opened up a whole new world for her. She had not realized that the seahorses she saw tend to mate for long durations, parading around their three-dimensional realm in pairs, with the dads taking on the job of incubating the eggs in a special pouch unique to the males. Or that many kinds of butterfly fish, abundant in the Keys, also tend to mate for keeps. Aptly named for their brilliant yellow-and-black markings and manner of fluttering about tropical reefs worldwide, most nibble and munch on bits of coral and sponge using their slender noses to probe where fish with less-well-endowed proboscises can't venture.

Since the Keys' designation as a marine sanctuary, there have been continual attempts to balance actions that may be destructive in nature, such as fishing, taking of coral, treasure hunting, and mining, with what is not, such as swimming, diving, boating, and provision of beauty and balm for the soul.

U.S. Secretary of Commerce in 1995, Ron Brown, provided what seems to be an unassailable rationale for having strong protective policies: "Nowhere is the marine environment more closely tied to the economy than in the Florida Keys." There, economy is based on tourists who come for the pure pleasure of experiencing the benign climate, the recreational opportunities, the chance to experience winter warmth, midsummer breezes, and a year-round, shoes-off atmosphere. Spencer Slate, who operates a dive center in Key Largo puts it simply: "A healthy environment means success: That's the bottom line. It means I can continue to make a living for myself and my employees."

Not everyone was pleased with the idea of establishing a sanctuary in the Florida Keys. Robust opposition came from treasure hunters, jet skiers, sport and commercial fishermen, and others fearing constraints on "traditional freedoms." Vested interests are so varied and so well established in some parts of the Florida Keys that it is difficult to enlist support for protective measures, despite the promise of long-term benefits. For instance, when a proposal to not take fish and other creatures within 20 percent of the sanctuary was advanced, proponents were burned in effigy—despite convincing evidence that such "no take" zones would help restore depleted species. Finally, in 1997, a lopsided compromise was reached: It allowed less than two percent to be set aside where fish, lobsters, and other marine life are fully protected.

However, there is growing interest in the no-take potential for the relatively pristine ocean surrounding a remote cluster of seven tiny islands 70 miles west of Key West, known as the Dry Tortugas. The islands offer a wealth of historic intrigue and natural beauty. Ponce de Leon encountered the islands in the 1500s while searching for the fabled Fountain of Youth. Centuries later, during the Civil War, a fort was constructed on one, Garden Key, to guard the Straits of Florida. The fort also served as a prison, including confinement of the physician, Samuel Mudd, punished for treating the injuries of President Lincoln's assassin, John Wilkes Booth. One island was home to a famous marine laboratory for the Carnegie Institution. Others have been grazed by cattle, and fishermen have stopped by many to take sea turtles, for whom the islands are named. For ages, all the Tortugas have served as safe havens for nesting seabirds.

Protection for the Dry Tortugas and their waters, and accompanying historic and natural wealth, began in 1935 when a (continued on page 76)

Not all corals are reef builders. The sea fans sprouting here like
flattened shrubs are among the many soft corals and gorgonians that thrive
in warm seas and are commonly associated with stony-reef corals. Both kinds benefit
from the same movable feast: the continual flow of plankton.

POPULATION
EXPLOSION

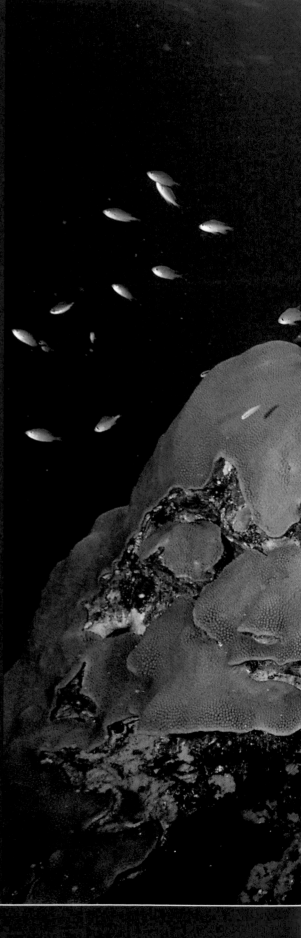

ONCE A YEAR, a few days after
the last full moon of summer,
many reef corals spawn. Most
eggs are released into the open sea;
a few become food for creatures such
as the scarlet brittle star, below,
tucking a sphere into its mouth
with one flexible arm. Like a glossy
green carpet, the coral mound at

right seems to flow over the reef.
In slow motion, this is just what
it does as new growth along its
margins gradually adds substance to
the reef. Minute plants growing in
the coral's tissue provide sustenance
for the expanding animal colony and
shelter for the plants, making for an
effective and enduring partnership.

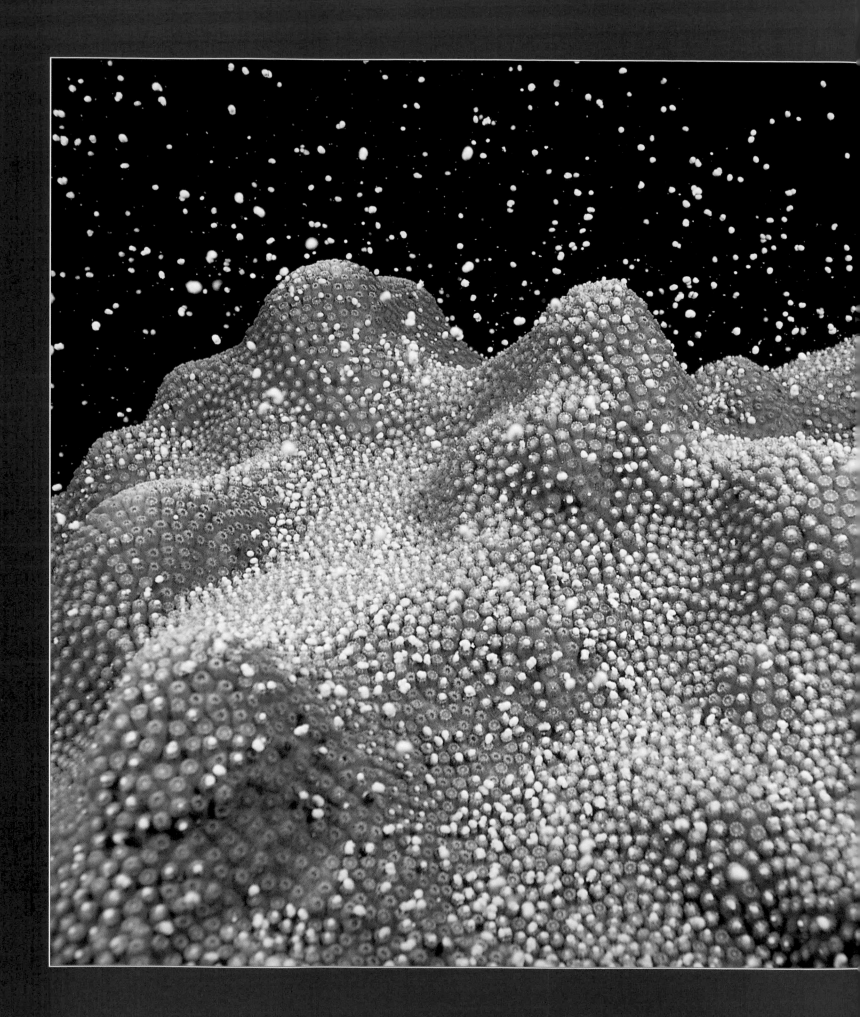

All heaven breaks loose as one coral, Montastraea faveolata, *left, at Flower Garden Banks releases eggs en masse and in concert with thousands of other coral mounds. Scientists, above, capture egg samples to study; fish feast on them.*

Greg Bunch, staff diver for the Aquarium of the Americas in New Orleans, and a frequent visitor to the Flower Garden Banks Sanctuary, recently witnessed coral spawning there.

Glancing over the side of a small boat more than a hundred miles south of Galveston, Texas, he shouted, "There are eggs on the surface! They're spawning!"

He continued, "I shone my light on the surface of the warm Gulf waters. Within its beam sparkled the tiny, jewel-like egg bundles which tell of events unfolding below…. I descended into clear waters filled with millions of rising egg bundles…."

Other reef residents, from sponges to mollusks to certain starfish, spawn at about the same time as the coral; thus critical elements for a new reef community travel together via plankton, express to new locations.

Almost any hard surface—a bottle, a feather, the steel legs of an oil platform—can provide firm footing for many creatures who otherwise could not survive. Fish are attracted to rigs, as are divers, who are sure to find spectacular communities of life prospering in the open sea around offshore platforms. Divers and boaters are not always welcome around active, working rigs, but the fish, turtles, and dolphins have a standing invitation. Rig operators and several oil companies in the Gulf of Mexico have developed congenial working partnerships with the Flower Garden Banks National Marine Sanctuary, including Stetson Bank, to develop special research and monitoring programs. Such arrangements reinforce the growing awareness that economic and environmental interests cannot only be compatible; they are inseparable.

Lights from an oil rig near Flower Garden Banks, above, glow like stars on the water's surface; underwater, divers, opposite, inspect a vertical reef blossoming from a rig's legs.

Astronaut Michael Collins often explores the mangrove-fringed shores of the Florida Keys Sanctuary, opposite, and finds pink conchs, below, for whom local residents are nicknamed. Collins says, "Walking trees, mangroves are called, and indeed their roots seem to be parading through the shallows. I love walking with them, watching, and listening. Roosting birds above, darting minnows below, everywhere mangroves go a profusion of life seems to follow."

FOLLOWING PAGES: *Hundreds of hammerhead sharks congregate in a warm-water system. Despite the common fear, humans are rarely attacked by sharks. However, millions of them are taken by us for food every year.*

115-square-mile area encompassing the seven tiny islands was designated as a National Monument. Now in the National Park System, the area offers birds and other wildlife protection on land, in the air, and in a narrow band of adjacent sea. But the surrounding ocean, now within the National Marine Sanctuary Program, until recently has been wide open for exploitation by fishermen.

The United States and other nations must protect a substantial fraction of the seafloor from trawling and other fishing methods. We need to protect these no-take reserves as strongly as we protect our National Parks, and we need to start doing it now!

TED DANSON
PRESIDENT, AMERICAN OCEANS CAMPAIGN

David Holtz, a longtime scientist with the Center for Marine Conservation, points out, "If any place in the Florida Keys should be fully protected, it's here. The way the currents flow from the Caribbean past the Tortugas and on into the Gulf of Mexico, larvae of many creatures, including young fish and coral, are swept from here to distant depleted areas, replenishing them. Despite growing pressures, the water quality and the abundance and diversity of life in the Tortugas reefs are about as pristine as any in the world."

Billy Causey, a former commercial fishermen who is now superintendent of the Florida Keys National Marine Sanctuary, believes that special ecological reserves such as this are vital to provide natural spawning, nursery, and permanent residence areas for the replenishment of marine life. He says, "By creating an ecological reserve in the sanctuary's portion of the Tortugas, we hope to preserve the extraordinary range of species found there. The reserve will also serve as a control site away from the populated Keys, helping scientists determine which changes in the coral reef ecosystem stem from human activities and which are natural." Protecting the Dry Tortugas does not mean that the place will be off-limits to visitors. Rather, it means that those who come should do so with the same spirit of respect that is afforded other national treasures: Glacier National Park, Yellowstone, the Smoky Mountains.

John Ogden, a marine scientist who has spent more time underwater on coral reefs than many fish, is spearheading a long-term study of the Tortugas area to see if the benefits of full protection can be quantified. Scientists with the Sustainable Seas Expeditions, using new technologies in collaboration with Ogden, hope to gain new insights into causes of the widespread decline of reef corals, and to find remedies. "Mangroves, seagrass beds, upstream sources of pollution, and wholesale taking of fish all influence the health of the reefs," he says. "Saving what remains...is critical to the restoration of those in trouble."

Archie Carr, known worldwide as the articulate "turtle man" for his lifetime of work on the biology and conservation of sea turtles, was optimistic over the state of nature and man in Florida. He observed, "One favorable development outweighs all the rest: It is a change in the heart of the people...an assessment of the trends would show the rate of loss being overtaken by the growth of a system of ecological ethics, by a new public consciousness and conscience."

I witnessed the power of these ethics in action in the late 1980s during a heated exchange of words about two small patches of surprisingly tropical reef in the northern Gulf of Mexico that were soon to be designated as a national marine sanctuary. Known as the Flower Garden Banks, the reefs are perched in 60 to 150 feet of water at the very tops of salt domes arising from deep water, 110 miles south of the Texas and Louisiana coasts.

Warm, highly saline water from the Caribbean sweeps past the Dry Tortugas northward into the Gulf, looping along the coasts of Yucatan, Texas, Louisiana, Mississippi, Alabama, and Florida, holding a certain integrity against the fresh water streaming from many rivers and bearing hosts of creatures at ease the year around in their tepid envelope, even as inshore winter temperatures drop below freezing. Awash in this current, life at the Flower Gardens seems to move to a calypso beat. Even at the surface, where the sea shades from indigo to emerald, there is often a tropical tang to the air, although the nearest coral reefs are hundreds of miles away—south in the Florida Keys, or south and west along the coast of Yucatan, or eastward across Florida in the Bahamas.

The almost-island Flower Garden reefs are healthy, teeming metropolises. The reefs provide natural hard surfaces within the range of life-giving sunlight, a bonanza for millions of small plants and invertebrates that must attach to something to get a start in life—from bacteria and seaweed, to coral, barnacles, sponges, starfish, and minute worms. These life-forms pass along a flow of energy that fuels thousands of small damselfish, schools of slender cigar minnows, and larger fish that in turn feed on them—snapper, grouper, sharks, and barracuda. Turtles stop by to browse on sponges; and manta rays circle over the reeftops like great moths, dwarfing divers lucky enough to be there at the right time. The frequent presence of whale sharks, the largest fish in the sea, suggests that they may come deliberately, not as chance riders on warm currents. The reefs jutting up in the middle of the ocean may serve as a reference point, a meeting place, a draw for them just as it is for thousands of divers and snorkelers.

Only yards away from this wonderland are dozens of oil wells, and thus the lively discussion I attended—mostly to listen. One oil company needed to transport hydrocarbons from the nearby well sites, and wanted to build a pipeline between the reefs. The proposed pipeline would likely do no harm to the reefs themselves if no leakage occurred, but the construction involved would be disruptive, and the idea generally seemed inconsistent with the image of what a marine sanctuary should be. An observer sized up the problem succinctly:

"Putting a pipeline through there.... Well, it would be like running a highway through the Louvre or a bridge across the Grand Canyon. It might make good sense in terms of getting from here to there, but still wouldn't be the right thing to do." The debate went on without resolution that day and for many months, but in the end the line was built around not between the reefs, and while the initial cost may have been greater, much goodwill was won. Since then, friendships have been forged between those who look after the reefs and do research there and those whose job it is to extract oil and gas from the surrounding seabed. In addition, the awareness of this hidden paradise has substantially increased.

Eighty feet under the surface of the Gulf of Mexico
heavenly bodies light our way across the sandflat…
coral polyps wave their dainty tentacles hungrily…
a large nurse shark glides past, her body shimmering, leaving in her wake
a tiny fireworks show.

EMMA HICKERSON
RESEARCH COORDINATOR, FLOWER GARDEN BANKS MARINE SANCTUARY

An area around the Flower Garden reefs—and the reefs themselves—was designated early in 1992 as a national marine sanctuary, and later Stetson Bank was added. The place is a popular recreational destination, with boatloads of snorkelers and divers often making weekend excursions in the hope that they might have a chance to school with a hundred or so hammerhead sharks during seasonal visits, or get up close and personal with minute, goggle-eyed gobies, tight formations of crevalle jacks, or large but gentle spotted morays.

Some people go to great lengths to be submerged, cameras ready and senses fine-tuned to witness the venerable phenomenon that is for coral and many other reef residents what certain days in springtime are to birds, bees, flowers, trees, and even to us. For several kinds of coral at the Flower Gardens, the magical moment typically arrives at about 9 p.m. Texas time, after the last full moon of summer, in late August or early September. Some people say they are drawn to the sea at this place and time because there and then their hearts pound to the beat of distant music, the memory of steel drums resounding through

Caribbean-clear night water. Others can't resist the adventure as they slide into a dark sea, neck hairs rising unbidden, pulses racing, echoing the urgent, ancient rhythms of the universe below. Some come as scientists, intent on understanding how and why and when what creature does what.

All hover mid-water or carefully kneel, glancing from their watches to the coral, awaiting the instant when on some silent cue all heaven breaks loose as millions of egg clusters burst from the embrace of soft tissues that have held them growing, ripening, for weeks. Clouds of sperm jet from coral mounds; small red brittle stars stand on tiptoe, arch their slender bodies, and send their own genetic messengers into the night-dark sea. Before dawn, even as opportunistic browsers feast on the sudden nutritious abundance, certain sponges, sea worms, mollusks and others give forth their own would-be offspring to a mostly uncertain future. In warm seas around the world at times just right for the creatures of the reef, the scene is repeated—but with thousands of subtle differences. This remains the same: Everywhere, crowds await the moment with the wonder of children.

If calm days follow, golden-orange rafts of fertilized eggs and swiftly developing larvae of corals, sponges, echinoderms, annelids, crustacea, mollusks, and more—together representing a fair cross section of reef dwellers—are thrown like gamblers' dice for ocean currents and happenstance to do what they will with them. A spoonful of the drifting mass properly planted could yield an infant reef, which of course is what happens when conditions are just right. Like seeds from fields and forests blown far and wide by storms, some settle and prosper, destined to colonize new areas or restore damaged places, while others are simply recycled as some creature's tasty morsel.

North of Australia and far west of Hawaii, nestled within an eroded volcanic crater along Tutuila Island, in American Samoa, lies a tiny but valuable gem: one-quarter square mile of coral reef and surrounding sea known as the Fagatele Bay National Marine Sanctuary. Of all the U.S. marine sanctuaries, it is the farthest west—thousands of miles more distant than Hawaii from continental North America; the farthest south—14 degrees below the Equator; and the smallest. Yet this toehold in the far Pacific is, in a way, much like one of the tiny bits of new life its reefs generate each year—a distant seed sprouting an intriguing concept. Many wonder what good it does to set aside a miniscule piece of reef as a sanctuary when there are so many reefs throughout the vast Pacific—a body of water that does, after all, encompass half the world.

Size aside, since designation in 1986 Fagatele Bay has been seriously ravaged by two major hurricanes and still shows the 1970s impact of large, voracious, coral-consuming starfish, the notorious crown-of-thorns. Overfishing is

TURTLE WATCH

AT SEA for most of their lives— as long as a hundred years— sea turtles retain a link to the land when they come ashore to nest. How do turtles sense where they are in the open sea, or know when to veer off an ocean highway to return time and again to a certain beach or speck of land on shore? Turtle expert Archie Carr uncovered some clues that helped him begin to make sense of turtle migrations, but he admitted that the ways of turtles are still mysterious. Among the most beloved residents of warm seas, all five kinds of sea turtles have become scarce due to deliberate taking for food, disruption and loss of their nests, and incidental capture in fishing nets. So serious is the decline that turtles have full protection in U.S. waters and varying degrees of protection around the world. Marine sanctuaries provide and protect feeding grounds, and they are places where people meet these charismatic creatures face to face.

Turtles attract tag-alongs such as surgeonfish, opposite, who graze on seaweed growing on the shell; other scavengers take "crumbs" as the turtle dines. At Gray's Reef, top, researcher Alex Score captures an injured loggerhead dubbed "Humpty-Dumpty." After healing, Humpty was released and tracked by satellite. Above, a young loggerhead is measured and marked by sanctuary personnel Chris Ostrom and Emma Hickerson before being released.

a large problem. Some would call this a disaster; others, notably sanctuary manager Nancy Daschbach, see unprecedented opportunity to showcase in a microcosm the problems that confront the world at large, and to promote solutions. Says she, "Fagatele Bay is a living laboratory, a place where human and natural pressures can be observed and evaluated at close range over a long time."

Symbiosis is the name of the game on the reef.
The signature group, the coral themselves, live intimately with their symbionts
in an almost science-fiction relationship: Jawfish share condos with shrimp;
anemone house some fish; crabs house some anemones; eels are
followed by jacks—and not as the supper item.

NANCY DASCHBACH
SANCTUARY MANAGER, FAGATELE BAY MARINE SANCTUARY

Besides village outreach programs, the bay is the site of repeated coral reef surveys, monitoring programs, and research on post-storm recovery. Many make a living catering to snorkelers, divers, and others who bring goodwill and take away only fine memories. In short, Fagatele Bay is a place where ideas of care are being planted and an ethic is growing that acknowledges what Polynesian cultures have known and lived for thousands of years: We must protect and respect the systems that sustain us; we must strike a balance between using a resource, and using it up, if we ourselves are to prosper.

From American Samoa to Hawaii in the Pacific, from the Gulf of Mexico to the Florida Keys to Gray's Reef in the Atlantic, and throughout all warm seas beyond, certain familiar faces reappear. Among them are the five main kinds of turtles, who range the world's warm oceans much as globe-trotting humans range over many lands. Some travel over a quarter of the planet while riding ocean currents, assisted now and then with deliberate thrusts of their hydrodynamically adept flippers. Envy the seafaring turtle who packs within her scaly hide all the ingredients needed for a century of doing whatever turtles do with their lives: find food, mates, places to nest and rest, but mostly travel, unerringly returning over decades to the same places, and, without language, passing along to new generations the cues needed to repeat the same tricks.

How do turtles sense where they are in the open sea, or know precisely when to veer off an ocean highway to return time and again to a certain beach along the shore of a speck of land that to non-turtles looks pretty much like hundreds of other beaches? Archie Carr, after a lifetime of searching, was excited by clues that helped him make some sense of turtle migrations, but admitted in his later years that the ways of turtles are still largely mysterious. What is known for sure is that nothing in the long and durable history of turtles has prepared them for the ways we now threaten their existence.

Sanctuaries enhance the chances for sea turtle survival by protecting critical habitats; they are also places where people can be inspired to care about turtles through personal encounters. Whether sea turtles survive to the end of the 21st century will be determined largely by conscious actions taken in the next few years. Slim, young, dark-haired biologist Alex Score often sees loggerhead turtles during monitoring visits to Gray's Reef, and captures and tags them to better understand their migrations. In the summer of 1998 she saw a young female in trouble, her shell cracked stem to stern. "She must have been dropped," Alex said, "…probably from a fishermen's net when it was winched onto the deck. She was lively—I nearly missed scooping her into my hand net—but I didn't have much hope that she could survive such a terrible wound."

Weeks later, after loving care and suitable medication in Marineland, Florida, the put-back-together turtle, dubbed Humpty-Dumpty, was released. Children and adults gathered on the dock at Sapelo, Georgia, and cheered as the lid was opened and clear, brown turtle eyes studied the situation. Attached to her back was a radio transmitter, which Alex explained: "We often see loggerheads at Gray's Reef, but aren't sure where they come from or where they're heading."

Reed Bohne leaped into the water and positioned himself strategically, immediately in front of the turtle to capture on film her historic return to the sea. The front of the crate slid open and Humpty-Dumpty blinked once. Then, a turtle transformed, she vaulted from the box with a thump and thrust of all flippers, in a flash erasing all doubt of impaired vigor.

"So much for their reputation for being slow," Bohne muttered, his finger still poised over the untouched "on" button.

I called a few days later to see if the tracking system was working, and Bohne gave me a jubilant update: "She went straight north for a hundred miles without stopping; then, after some circling around, maybe to get her bearings, she headed straight back. Guess where she is now? Gray's Reef! She came right to the place where Alex captured her and is hanging out there right now."

Humpty-Dumpty's trail was a hot item on the Internet for months, with school kids calling in and newspapers and television stations reporting her progress. Like dolphins and whales, turtles are becoming recognized as individuals through whose eyes we can see ourselves more clearly. As Humpty-Dumpty travels through the warm seas of the future, she and her mended shell serve as a symbol of a new and growing ethic of caring.

Fagatele Bay, in American Samoa, opposite, is a small but significant tropical lagoon protected since 1986 as a U.S. Marine Sanctuary. Among the many residents of its coral reefs are clownfish and their anemone partners, at top. Above, a voracious beauty with an appetite for living coral, the crown-of-thorns starfish is a natural member of healthy Pacific reefs, but when abundant, can cause swift and lasting damage.

FOLLOWING PAGES: "Diving with humpbacks is incredible," says co-author Wolcott Henry. "They can be as large as buses.... Fortunately they are also remarkably aware of divers, and agile enough to avoid direct contact."

Warm tropical seas splashing
on palm-fringed shores, magnificent
sunsets, and silken breezes entice
visitors to the island of Maui, adjacent
to the Hawaiian Humpback
Whale Sanctuary. Such conditions
attract many to this and
other warm-water destinations,
including the Florida Keys
and American Samoa—places with
thriving marine sanctuaries.

IN COLD WATERS

IN COLD WATERS

I TURNED MY HEAD just in time to see a sleek, spray-sheathed 40-ton body blast out of the sea. A humpback whale, one of several that for an hour had cruised along Boston's Stellwagen Bank near the New England Aquarium's research vessel and whale-watching boat, *Voyager II,* had decided to do that amazing thing that whales do—leap nearly aloft, down, then aloft again, and again. No one knows why they do it…although somebody in the crowd suggested that this whale, "After hours of stuffing himself with fish, might be shaking 'em down, making room for dessert."

With a remote camera fastened to a sled-like underwater vehicle, we tried to catch a whale in the act of scooping up its dinner, but succeeded only in seeing tantalizing glimpses of the slender, wraith-like fish the whales were after—sand lances, colored so like the pale sand they dived into as to appear invisible but for their bright black eyes and occasional flashes of steel-blue iridescence. Clouds of them emerged and swam in close formation, plunging for cover when startled by the lights or bump of the machine as it moved across their rippled gravel-and-sand domain.

Whale-watching has become a multimillion-dollar enterprise
for people in many of the marine sanctuaries. Revenue raised by whales alive
far exceeds the value of whales when taken as commodities.

PRECEDING PAGES: *In a single gulp, a humpback whale near Stellwagen Bank
National Marine Sanctuary scoops up thousands of gallons of seawater seething with
small fish. Pushing its great tongue against brushlike baleen, the whale forces water
out, but keeps in the food for a midday meal. Enterprising gulls snag the scraps.*

Humpbacks feeding at the surface do so obviously—jaws agape, sometimes in unison, sometimes singly, but always impressively. When krill or small fish are their targeted food, the whales often encircle their tiny prey, concentrating them with streams of bubbles, then rise through the middle of the bubble-net, mouths wide open. Just as people are entranced watching elephants, lions, and zebras go through their paces on the African savanna, so are thousands now attracted to watch ocean wildlife on this 842 square miles of open sea above a submerged bank formed by the retreat of glaciers at the end of the last ice age. Below the surface are rocky ledges, boulder fields, muddy basins, and broad expanses of sand and gravel harboring scallops, northern lobster, flounder, cod, and much more, including, of course, seals and whales that dive down to dine.

Cool-water systems, such as Stellwagen Bank, and on the West Coast—Monterey, the Channel Islands, Cordell Bank, and the Olympic Coast—are shaped by cold currents. All are nutrient-rich and highly productive places, giving rise to large populations of small fish and crustaceans. These in turn yield enormous numbers of commercially valuable fish and marine mammals such as the humpbacks.

When not sleeping, humpback whales feed almost nonstop during the summer months, stoking their great bodies with energy needed to grow thick layers of blubber. The subcutaneous fat not only helps keep them warm in New England's cool waters, it also serves as fuel when they migrate south to the tropics in winter months, where good meals for baleen whales are few and far between. After months of feeding, humpbacks appear to fast until they return again to where food is plentiful and available in concentrated masses.

Their migration from Stellwagen Bank and nearby waters to nursery and breeding areas in the Dominican Republic's Silver Bank Sanctuary is tracked by researchers who have named, photographed, and cataloged hundreds of individual whales in recent years. The pattern is similar to what humpbacks do on the West Coast, traveling at the end of summer from cold, food-rich areas along the coast of Alaska to Hawaii's tropical seas, then back again in late spring. It works for humpbacks, having their cool dining areas separated from warm nurseries by thousands of miles, but most sea creatures must spend their entire lives in water that, to us, is inhospitably cold all the time.

Even in warm-water systems, surface warmth soon gives way to the chill that characterizes deep seas everywhere. One day in 1979 at high noon in Hawaii, I experienced this transition for myself when I descended in a one-person diving system called *Jim,* strapped to the front of the University of

Hawaii's research sub, *Star II.* I passed through warm, well-lit surface waters into the realm where whales routinely dive, where light is a whisper, a faint glow far above, like the sky just before dawn or the faintly illuminated heavens just before stars appear. As I descended, my metal suit felt increasingly like a walking refrigerator. Water temperature on the surface was 27°C (81°F); at 1,250 feet, it was 40 degrees cooler. Had I descended another thousand feet, as sperm whales often do, I would have entered that great mass of water that holds its enormous cargo of life in a near-freezing embrace.

In cold-water systems the temperature change is less dramatic from surface to depths. In New England, ice forms in places along the coast during winter months, floating above the less frigid liquid ocean below. Offshore the sea stays unfrozen, but the pace of life slows. In winter there is less sunlight and warmth to drive the photosynthetic processes that support the area's productivity. Still creatures abound. While fishermen, says author Mark Kurlansky, are bundled in layers of protective gear, "Cod," he remarks, "like the...water because...7°C (45°F) is a cod's idea of warm...."

"The creatures of Stellwagen are as spectacular, varied, and abundant as those of the more recognized Serengeti or Yellowstone National Parks. Yet, far from distant or remote, the Stellwagen wilderness thrives only 26 miles from the Boston metropolitan area.

JERRY R. SCHUBEL
PRESIDENT, NEW ENGLAND AQUARIUM

For centuries the Grand Banks, Georges Bank, Stellwagen Bank, and other parts of the eastern North Atlantic yielded a good living to fishermen from several nations from the taking of *Gadus morhua,* the Atlantic cod, and other bottom-dwelling groundfish—pollock, haddock, hake, and flounder. But especially the cod. Known widely as "king cod" because of its powerful role in driving the prosperity of New England for generations, this resilient fish has been subdued by a combination of *(continued on page 104)*

FOLLOWING PAGES: *Many have come to love the sculpted shorelines, the stacked and weathered rocks, and the craggy cliffs of the Olympic Coast. Bob Steelquist, education director for the sanctuary there observes, "The land of the coast is a land of voices...the voices of the forest, the voices of the breakers...the voices of time...."*

Crimson anemones, orange starfish, pale sponges, and multishaded coral thrive on
the crest of Cordell Bank, a mountain that rises from the ocean floor to 115 feet below the
surface. Those who venture to the 562-square-mile sanctuary 60 miles northwest
of San Francisco can join several species of whales and visit the spot where more species
of albatrosses have been seen than anywhere else in the Northern Hemisphere. Divers, such
as this researcher surveying benthic—deepwater—animals, consider Cordell Bank
a living laboratory and an Olympian goal: a mountain to climb from the top down.

More than 150 years ago, Richard Henry Dana observed in his book Two Years Before the Mast *that "Monterey…is decidedly the pleasantest and most civilized place in California." Yet Dana was unaware of the spectacular beauty hidden beneath the sea he sailed—from kelp forests to canyons. The 5,328-square-mile Monterey Bay Sanctuary now encompasses the bay and extends into coastal waters north and south.*

FOLLOWING PAGES:
Otters, the widely loved clowns-of-the-sea, have staged an encouraging recovery around Monterey Bay since the 1800s, when they were nearly exterminated in California for their soft fur coats.

pressures, mostly because for too long, too many of us have consumed too many of them. By the 1990s the collapse of cod and other groundfish, and the coincident plight of fishermen and fish helped spur the dedication of Stellwagen Bank as a marine sanctuary. Although not off-limits to fishing, the sanctuary is the focal point for efforts to develop an integrated network of marine-protected areas within the Gulf of Maine, involving the U.S. and Canada.

Designated as part of the National Marine Sanctuary System in 1992, the area was recently renamed to honor an outspoken advocate of ocean research and protection, retired Massachusetts Congressman Gerry Studds. The Gerry E. Studds Stellwagen Bank Sanctuary is only 25 miles from Boston, and 3 miles from Cape Ann or Provincetown, and thus easily within the range of people who come out for the day, bring a lunch, and in the summer catch glimpses of feeding humpbacks, occasionally a finback whale, or even one of the rarest animals on Earth—the northern right whale. They and other marine mammals, as well as numerous seabirds—gulls, storm petrels, and northern gannets—are drawn to the abundant populations of fish, which in turn are attracted to small crustaceans, worms, and other invertebrates, which are powered by phytoplankton that abounds in cool-water systems with legendary richness.

The wealth was evident from our perches on the *Voyager II*. The remote camera relayed images from 150 feet below that were bathed in a pea-green haze, presenting a close-up view of what we could expect to see on a grand scale at the surface: This rich broth of an ocean gives rise to high productivity and a multilayered food web that begins with single-celled microalgae and ultimately powers some of the largest creatures on the planet—from bluefin tuna to great whales. I was tempted to jump in and and see for myself what the terrain below was like, but the depth was beyond comfortable diving range with scuba tanks, and the water cold enough to require a sturdy protective suit. "Next time," I thought, "I'll be back, and I'll be ready to look around using a cozy, warm, dry submarine."

Plans are under way to do just that as part of the Sustainable Seas Expeditions. Research for the Expeditions is being carried out in all the sanctuaries, but the cold-water sanctuaries are the testing grounds for an exciting new vehicle. Dozens of researchers have been trained to pilot the newly developed *DeepWorker* submersibles, which look rather like small cars, and can descend to 2,000 feet—deep enough to explore well beyond the now-submerged parts of the continent that were once dry land.

Peter Auster, one of the pilot-scientists, has already invested years exploring New England waters and is now the science director of the National Undersea Research Center at the University of Connecticut. Often he deploys remote-operated camera systems to find out the nature of the life below and to look at the effects of various kinds of fishing gear on the ecosystems—especially the impact of trawls that scrape the ocean floor. Eager to make on-the-spot observations, Auster says, "I just want to sit on the bottom and see what happens—maybe even stay overnight out there. People camp in the woods all the time. Why not camp on Stellwagen Bank, 300 feet down?"

Sitting inside *Deep Worker* is not quite like curling up in a sleeping bag under the stars. But the air inside the little sub is maintained at comfortable surface pressure; there is room to pack a midnight snack; and the view seems cosmic when minute luminous creatures brush against the sub's clear dome, each emitting an eerie blue-green flash or glow.

In the ocean realm…every time we break its surface
to probe within, we are at the mercy of the unexpected….
It's adventure! It's discovery! It's exploration!

STEVE GITTINGS
Science Coordinator, NOAA Sanctuaries and Reserves Division

Another aim of the Sustainable Seas Expeditions is to explore, research, and develop a program of education involving teachers and students for all the nation's marine sanctuaries. One of my first goals was to go to each of the sanctuaries, to meet with their staff, with researchers, and with youngsters who, after all, will have to cope with the consequences of decisions now being made about the nation's natural resources. I began with a cool-water sanctuary.

In May 1998, soon after the official launch of the project, I flew from Seattle in a small plane to Port Angeles, Washington, headquarters for the 3,310-square-mile Olympic Coast National Marine Sanctuary. This protected area encompasses a stretch of rugged coastline from just east of Cape Flattery southward to the mouth of the Copalis River, and seaward 35 miles. Designated during the administration of President William Clinton in 1994, the sanctuary teams with the National Park Service to provide on-site education programs for visitors and students, and works with local Makah, Quileute, Hoh, and Quinault tribes in developing opportunities for economic use of the region's natural resources on a sound, sustained basis.

Few places on Earth are as spectacularly beautiful as the rocky, wave-swept shoreline of the Pacific Northwest. Bob Steelquist, education director for the Olympic Coast Sanctuary and father of two young boys who love to explore, writes of Washington's coast: "You know you are approaching by the sound—a whisper at first, a hiss…The land of the coast is a land of voices…of the forest…of the breakers…of time. Water-worn pebbles gurgle as they roll in the frothy surf. Sea lions bark. There are the voices of canoe bailers; whale, seal, and salmon hunters; gatherers of clams; singers."

Many have come to love the coast's improbable-looking stacked and weathered rocks, craggy cliffs, and sculpted shorelines, from people who settled thousands of years ago, to venturesome Europeans who came merely centuries ago, to those who are truly recent arrivals. Every year millions of visitors are drawn to the wild Olympic Coast's beauty of land and sea, but few who come here have experienced the equally grand panorama that shapes the depths below: submerged volcanoes, hydrothermal vents, steep canyons, and a vast and fertile submerged ancient coastal area. Only a few submersibles have ventured to a few places, allowing a few people to have a brief look at the nature of the undersea realms that make life possible for seals, sea lions, whales, birds—and people. That may soon change.

To me the most important role of the Olympic Coast Sanctuary is to ensure that
all future generations…experience the Olympic Coast we enjoy today.
Ultimately, for a sanctuary to be successful, the local community must accept the national
marine sanctuary concept…to take ownership and see it as "their sanctuary."

GEORGE GALASSO
ACTING MANAGER, OLYMPIC COAST MARINE SANCTUARY

The Sustainable Seas Expeditions program aims to enable many to have their first look at the canyons within the sanctuary, to film and document what is there, and with live broadcasts from underwater, share the view and the knowledge gained. There is also great interest in determining the effect fishing techniques have on underwater systems, just as there is in New England, and some of the proposed studies will look at such issues. Hard questions will be asked about what actions might be taken to maintain the health of the Olympic Coast and restore depleted ocean wildlife, such as the native salmon so vital to orca whales, eagles, bears, and local peoples.

Whatever the topics raised, none are likely to be as thoughtful as the questions asked by 40 middle school and high school *(continued on page 114)*

Twenty-five miles due west of San Francisco, the Farallon Islands—
and a cluster of rocky pinnacles—jut from the sea, above, creating an irresistible
attraction for seabirds and several kinds of marine mammals, as well as thousands
of recreational boaters, whale-watchers, and others. Some 1,255 square miles of
ocean around the islands were designated in 1981 as sanctuary.

FOLLOWING PAGES: *A famous resident of waters around the Farallon Islands is*
Carcarcadon carcharias, *the great white shark. More to be respected and
protected than feared, this large predator dines on fish
and large marine mammals, performing an ecosystem role for the ocean
much like that of lions, tigers, or wolves on land.*

Exploring California's four marine sanctuaries—all cool-water systems— provides opportunity for everyone. For divers, opposite, there are otherworldly scenes: a scattering of sea stars and deep kelp forests. For shoreline explorers, rocky tidal pools and shallow ocean abound with abalone, anemones, and crabs, below, top to bottom.

Youngsters get to know sea stars at the Monterey Sanctuary. Says Shelley Du Puy,
of the National Marine Sanctuary Program staff, "Never underestimate the impact you
have on the children. They are little bundles of potential, just waiting to experience
the wonders of the Earth." Below, a painted greenling rests next to an anemone.
Urchins, opposite, were once regarded as a threat to California's kelp forests because
of their appetite for the algae that grows there. Now they are threatened—
by the growing human appetite for them as culinary delights.

students who participated in a one-day "student summit" on the oceans sponsored by NOAA and the National Geographic Society during my May visit to Port Angeles. I led off with a "state of the oceans" summary, then received a barrage of pointed questions, some which taxed every ounce of ingenuity and stored knowledge in my brain: "What is this country doing to support ocean exploration?" "What effect is pollution having on the sea—and us?" "What causes the El Niño phenomenon?" "What new laws can help protect the ocean?" "What can be done about overfishing?" "Is ozone depletion affecting ocean plankton?" "Why don't people care as much about the ocean as they do about space?"

I tried turning the questions back to them—partly because I have earnestly been seeking answers to such questions myself, and was hoping for—and got—some new insights from the sharp young minds assembled. In some cases, answers are hard to come by, but the exciting, exhilarating, promising thing is that the questions were being asked.

I am keenly aware that those involved in student summits as the Sustainable Seas program progresses around the country will soon be leading expeditions themselves, and wrestling with the consequences of actions taken now. Like national parks, marine sanctuaries are part of a living legacy that can be maintained—or lost—depending on how people care for them. The students I met had no doubt of a promising future for the oceans—if the decisions are theirs.

More than a thousand miles south is one of the most mysterious, least known, wildest, hardest to imagine of all of the cold water sanctuaries—Cordell Bank, which lies 60 miles northwest of San Francisco. Embraced by the cold, southbound California Current, it is, in fact, a submerged island that rises to within 115 feet of the surface and drops off swiftly to depths greater than a mile. You can't see the place from the surface, let alone from the nearest land, but sailors have known of it for ages as a welcome anchorage, well offshore. Nutrient-rich deep water wells up along the sides of the island, setting in motion the familiar food chain: Microscopic plants and animals yield krill, jellies, and small fish, which in turn yield everything from rockfish, lingcod, and salmon, to Dall's porpoises, shearwaters, and pigeon guillemots. More species of albatross have been seen at Cordell Bank than anywhere else in the Northern Hemisphere. Whales—blue, humpback, minke, and gray—cruise the area, as do numerous sport and commercial fishermen, for similar reasons: food.

Scientists come, too, and mountain-climbing divers who don't mind starting at the top of the peak and working down. Using conventional diving methods, time is short and depth is strictly limited, usually to 130 feet or less. Robert Schmeider, an energetic scientist-explorer, led the move to win sanctuary status for Cordell Bank. He describes it as "a castle tower above a moat" perched at the very edge of the continental shelf where "the tops of the ridges are smothered in a fantastic jumble of sponges, anemones, hydrocorals, hydroids, tunicates, barnacles, crabs…." Formally designated in 1989, it has become for skilled divers an Olympian goal. For scientists it is a wondrous living laboratory, like a stationary research ship submerged in the open sea. There they find many species rare or unknown inshore. For the Sustainable Seas Expeditions, deploying the *DeepWorker* subs will make possible longer, deeper dives—and insights—than have heretofore been possible.

Anyone can go on a boat to visit the "liquid sky" above this mountain and revel in the gathering of birds, whales, and small creatures in the depths below. Ed Ueber, who manages the Cordell Bank and nearby Gulf of the Farallones Marine Sanctuaries, sums up the appeal for many: "The ocean flows with the soul of life, from abyss to estuarine shore…."

A few miles south of Cordell Bank and 25 miles due west of San Francisco, the Farallon Islands and a cluster of nearby rocky pinnacles jut from the sea, creating a spectacular attraction for seabirds and many kinds of marine mammals. Protected for many years because of their importance to wildlife—including sheltering the largest concentration of breeding seabirds in the continental United States—access to the islands is severely restricted. Steller's sea lions, California sea lions, elephant seals, fur seals, and harbor seals are among the 33 kinds of marine mammals for whom these waters are significant feeding or breeding grounds—or both. This fact, plus the desire to protect the area for the enjoyment of millions of recreational boaters, whale-watchers, and others, was among the reasons that 1,255 square miles of ocean surrounding the islands were designated in 1981 as the Gulf of the Farallones National Marine Sanctuary.

While seabirds and marine mammals are popular attractions, other notable creatures live in these waters, including several shark species—basking, blue, seven gill, and perhaps most notorious of all, the great white. Known to scientists as *Carcharadon carcharias,* to Australians as "white death" or sometimes "white pointer," in reference to their conical front end, the great white shark is an impressive predator that has been known to reach more than 20 feet in length and weigh more than three and a half tons.

When I see a shark in the sea, it's a sign that something is right about the place. To sustain a great predator, a system has to be healthy enough to produce recurring numbers of whatever lives there on many levels—with enough remaining for top carnivores to stay in business. By preferentially selecting for lunch the least nimble members of a community, white sharks and other large predators continually hone the sharp edge of what works. The Inuit say, "Wolves keep the caribou strong." At the Farallones and in the oceans worldwide, sharks are the wolves' equivalent—a vital part of the ecosystem.

Protection befitting the richness of America's oceans and shorelines demands a National Marine Sanctuary Program to safeguard the web of life in our seas for future generations.

KATHRYN FULLER
PRESIDENT, WORLD WILDLIFE FUND

Fortunately, the Farallon Islands still have their wild essence, sharks and all. That essence prevails along much of the coast of California, despite increasing pressures from some of the fastest growing population centers in the country. Numerous state and federal wilderness lands and parks have been established to protect and make available to the public the natural land heritage that might otherwise have been engulfed by other priorities, from shopping centers and housing developments to farms and industrial parks. Had the idea for national parks been set in motion in 1972 instead of 1872, many of the lands now cherished as natural treasures would surely be gone.

Recognizing this, there was a sense of urgency in the early 1990s about taking bold measures to establish a sanctuary in the sea south of San Francisco near Monterey, toward Big Sur. Several proposals were advanced, including one for a shoreline-hugging sanctuary of very modest size. The largest sanctuary would encompass more than 5,000 square miles, extend more than 35 miles offshore, and include rocky shores, sandy beaches, kelp forests, deep submarine canyons, and the open sea beyond.

As the newly appointed chief scientist of NOAA, I asked to see the basis for a small sanctuary versus a large one, and was not surprised when the reports made a scientific case for the largest proposal, an area that would encompass entire ecosystems and a significant portion of the range of certain sensitive species, including California's beloved sea otters. Roger McManus, president of the Center for Marine Conservation, said that he was confident that the people of California and the nation as a whole, if asked, would almost certainly favor the largest area, and he was right. Every public meeting was packed with citizens who overwhelmingly supported "big is better," and in September 1992, a ceremony honoring the Monterey Bay National Marine

Sanctuary—the newest, largest sanctuary—was held under a clear blue sky overlooking the rocky tidal pools bordering the Monterey Bay Aquarium.

David Packard, industrialist, former U.S. Deputy Secretary of Defense, philanthropist, and founder of the Aquarium, shared thoughts about his love of the sea, especially the Monterey-Big Sur area, now with a new "insurance policy" for the future. Sam Farr, today a Congressman representing the Monterey area, spoke movingly on behalf of himself and his constituents. Others had their say, each aware that a historic moment had arrived: An aroused, concerned public had made a difference by making their voices heard. But the most eloquent endorsement for the "big idea" came from the west, where a brisk sea breeze brought enthusiastic barks from a rowdy gang of sea lions, and from the sea a few feet from the crowd, where a young otter whistled softly.

Seeing the otter, I smiled, remembering the first such furry face I glimpsed years before in 1966, when I stopped along California's famous Highway 1 at Big Sur, overlooking a massive forest of giant kelp. At first I thought I might be mistaken, that the dark round object that caught my eye might be the bulbous top of *Nereocystis,* the bull kelp. But the lump disappeared in a wave— and reappeared with whiskers, paws, and brown belly attached. My first sighting was not far from where otters were "rediscovered" in the late 1930s, after their near-annihilation in California one hundred years earlier.

It took only a century, beginning with their discovery by Europeans in 1741, to turn all but a few into grist for the popular fur trade of the time. More than a million otter skins were taken for a market so important, economically, that it is said to be one of the justifications for the acquisition of California. The International Fur Treaty of 1911 banned further taking of otters, but by then, it appeared there were no more in California, anyway.

A few found a haven along the rugged Big Sur coastline, however. In 1938, when California's human population was less than 7 million, about 50 otters were found larking about in protected coves and kelp forests. Since then, otters and people have prospered, our population nearing 25 million; theirs, about 2,000.

Unlike seals, sea lions, and whales, sea otters have no protective layer of fat to keep them warm or tide them over during lean times. Two things enable them to stay warm year-round, despite their cold-water realm: a fast metabolism and a deep, soft, thick fur coat so well-groomed that they often resemble cats in hyperdrive. Historically, the otters' furry wraps have made them targets for taking; now, it's their imperative to eat that puts them at odds with people. Fishermen regard otters as competitors for *(continued on page 122)*

IN DEEP WATERS

ALL OF THE SEA is dark some of the time, but most of it, from about a thousand feet to the deepest ocean seven miles down, is cold and dark all of the time—except for the sparkle, flash, and glow of deep-sea creatures who manufacture their own, living light. "More than 80 percent of the animals in the deep sea have some form of bioluminescence," says marine scientist Bruce Robison. Using manned submersibles and undersea robots, Robison and his colleagues at the Monterey Bay Aquarium Research Institute and the nearby aquarium, for more than a decade have been exploring the secrets of Monterey Canyon, the largest coastal submarine canyon of the American continents, now contained within the Monterey Bay National Marine Sanctuary. "It's like having the Grand Canyon just offshore," says Robison. "Many who come to Monterey don't know what they're missing. Imagine going to the rim of the Grand Canyon and never looking over the edge." Speaking of the dark, mostly cold, high-pressure ocean realm below sunlit surface waters, Robison adds, "It's the largest and least explored

Three ways to go: As a diver, to 100 feet, here photographing salps; as a pilot of a Monterey Bay Aquarium Research Institute remotely operated vehicle, top, working thousands of feet down; or, below, as an observer in DeepWorker submersibles to 2,000 feet, here with designer Phil Nuytten and Sylvia Earle.

environment on Earth, and it's brimming with life." In 1999, National Geographic's Sustainable Seas Expeditions is giving researchers and educators new ways to venture to depths as great as 2,000 feet using innovative technologies, including the newly developed *DeepWorker* submersibles. Andrew Shepard, a NOAA engineer with years of experience with manned and robotic submersibles, is among the 65 researchers trained to use the new subs. As he prepared for his first check-out dive, Shepard recalls, "I was determined to be professional. I was here to objectively evaluate this system for use in scientific research, to consider the complexity and difficulty in driving the sub that might compromise use of that most valuable scientific tool, the brain. As I took my shoes off and prepared to enter *Deep-Worker,* I was professionally thinking, 'This is so cool!'" All the marine sanctuaries, America's national parks under the sea, will be explored using this and other new systems with support from the Goldman Foundation, the National Geographic Society, NOAA, and other private and federal agencies starting in 1999.

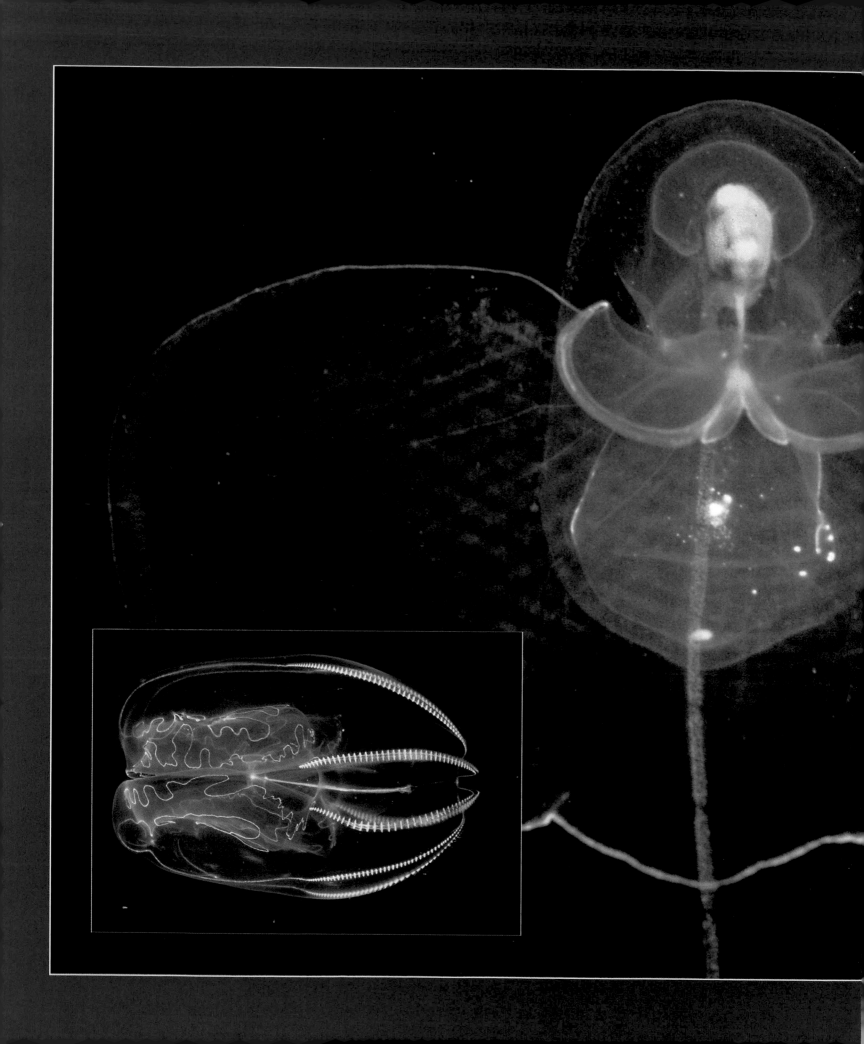

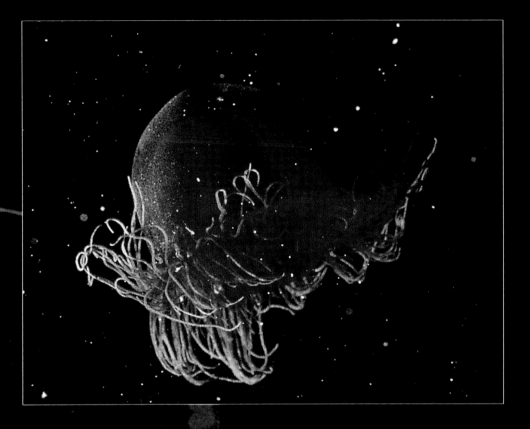

IN DEEP WATERS

Variations on the theme of jelly,
three distinct divisions of life soar through
deep waters. Far left, a ctenophore propels its frilly
self with eight bands of iridescent cilia;
at left, a luminous mollusk, in effect a snail with
a sail, gently powers its way through the sea.
Above, a mid-water jellyfish with a body
like a dollop of strawberry jam, pulses away
with flurried tentacles.

the crabs, clams, urchins, abalone, and other small creatures otters require to fuel their high-energy, warm-blooded lifestyle. After all, a 40-pound otter may consume 10 pounds of food a day—about 25 percent of its body weight. But otters do not take indiscriminately, and their diet does range over at least 45 different kinds of organisms, not just those favored by commercial fishermen.

Divers have reported watching otters underwater: the animals choose a rock with apparent care for its shape and size for the job at hand, use it to crack open a shell, then return it to its former location for later retrieval. Most of the energy gained is consumed catching their next meal or keeping warm or doing what some people think otters do best—fooling around. They seem to have mastered the art of play, rolling and tumbling with such pleasure that when I see two or three or six frolicking like puppies or small children, it takes considerable restraint on my part not to jump in and join them.

Long-term studies are beginning to provide new insights into relationships among otters and their habitat. One, for instance, gives evidence that in a healthy ecosystem, otters, with their varied diet of shellfish, help maintain the prosperity of kelp and other plants that in turn are vital as food and shelter for billions of creatures.

Just offshore from Santa Barbara, California, a still mostly wild ocean embraces the islands of San Miguel, Santa Rosa, Santa Cruz, Anacapa, and Santa Barbara—collectively known as California's Channel Islands. In 1980, during President Carter's administration, 1,658 square miles of ocean surrounding the islands were designated as a national marine sanctuary. It is one of the most popular places in the world for recreational boating, described in Fagan and Pomeroy's *Cruising Guide to the Channel Islands* as including "desolate anchorages, quiet coves, and magnificent offshore islands that have attracted explorers, missionaries, settlers, and tourists for centuries." It is also among the world's most popular undersea destinations.

Author Howard Hall knows why. After thousands of hours exploring and filming in California's undersea forests, he wrote in *Secrets of the Ocean Realm,* "When the water is clear and hundred-foot-high trees of giant kelp sway gently to the rhythm of waves and current, and when the amber twilight penetrating through the dense canopy far above reveals the carpet of fluorescent anemones and red gorgonian corals clinging to the reef below, to say that it is overwhelmingly beautiful is accurate but not adequate." Kelp forests are to the sea what redwoods are to the land—havens and sources of sustenance for thousands of creatures. A few strands of kelp may supply shelter and food for millions of small animal residents, submarine cities that far surpass nearby Los Angeles in terms of diversity and sheer numbers.

Among the most colorful members of the Channel Islands kelp communities—in personality as well as gaudy attire—is California's state marine fish, the garibaldi. Divers will tell you that despite their appealing, flowerlike appearance, ounce for ounce these fish along with most of their damselfish relatives are the feistiest in the sea. "If garibaldi were as big as blue sharks, no one would dare go in the ocean," said my son, Richie, after his first eye-to-eye encounter with one. Males, in particular, are extremely protective of their chosen patch of turf, a deliberately cultivated, manicured lawn of seaweed that is more pampered than the most tenderly-cared-for golfing green. If intruders such as hungry algae-eating urchins try to move in, the defending garibaldi grabs them by the spines and hustles them out of town, many yards away. Inquisitive divers have had their curiosity rewarded with a vigorous, head-on "bap" to the nose, chest, arm, or other imposing bits of anatomy.

The reason for passionate lawn care has a lot to do with courtship. A garibaldi's soft carpet of fine red algae is intended as a lure for potential mates and, in due course, as a nursery. When a mother-to-be swims by, the lawn-keeping male tries to woo her with loud clucking sounds and a series of acrobatic loops. If she's impressed with the display or otherwise interested in a particular garden, she may swim over and begin laying eggs. After a brief romantic interlude, garibaldi style, she will then leave, and thereafter, it is up to the male to tend the nest, defend it from marauding egg-eaters and other threats, and briefly protect the newly emerged fishlets.

From the forests of kelp just offshore to the deep-sea canyons beyond, the natural systems that are now encompassed by the system of cool-water sanctuaries on the nation's West Coast are the product of hundreds of millions of years of fine-tuning. Ice ages have come and gone; waves of extinction have eliminated some species and favored the growth of others.

People are thought to have arrived in the Channel Islands region 10,000 years ago, as the last ice age tapered into a warming trend. The Chumash, who numbered in the thousands at the peak of their culture, sustained themselves largely by taking ocean wildlife, by hunting birds and mammals, and by gathering wild plants. By the mid-1700s, Spanish pioneers had repeatedly visited the area and one, Pedro Fages, wrote that "the fishing is so good, and so great is the variety of fish…that this industry alone would suffice to provide sustenance to all the settlers which this vast stretch of country would receive." Millions of modern "settlers" no longer rely on wildlife for primary sources of food, but even so, much more is removed from the sea now than during any time in the past—millions of tons annually of squid, fish, crabs, clams, urchins, and other wildlife. That is why there is growing interest in having marine sanctuaries serve as a yardstick for measuring change, and as a source for restoring species in trouble.

Francesca Cava, first manager of the Channel Islands National Marine Sanctuary and later director of the entire National Marine Sanctuary Program, has been a galvanizing force in establishing education programs that involve the public in support of the sanctuaries and their resources. On her first post, at the Channel Islands, her authority and resources were limited, but she did have a 30-foot boat, the *Xantu,* at her disposal, and an agreement with the Santa Barbara Museum of Natural History to develop a small museum, the "Sea Center," to act as a window on Santa Barbara Channel. From there, she began to involve people, and the programs have become far-reaching.

In children she has found a special audience. "When I visited a local elementary school, I was surprised to see so many eyes sparkle as I described the treasures that lay beyond the shore: What's there? How do I visit? What can I do? Children seem to understand more readily than many adults that when abalone, cow cod, Guadalupe fur seals, and even slimy eels become less and less common, something is wrong, we should care, and we should act." From one class, called *Los Marineros,* or "The Mariners," taught in English and Spanish, Cava developed a curriculum focusing on the ocean, its treasures, and its needs. Today the program is part of the formal 5th and 6th grade curriculum for the Santa Barbara school system, in which children visit and volunteer at the sanctuaries. "I wish they would grow up faster," says Cava. "The sea needs their knowledge and caring."

In the meantime, however, the children are building their own legacy. Jean Michel Cousteau, long a resident of California, remembers as a child going with his father, explorer Jacques Cousteau, to many wild places and falling in love with the great diversity of life in pristine seas. But the consequences of overfishing, pollution, and increased human occupation of coastal areas have greatly altered much that Cousteau once took for granted. "So much has changed in my lifetime, I cannot take my own children to see places I knew and do things with them that my father and I did when I was a boy," he says. "Marine sanctuaries, if fully protected, offer hope that for the children of the future, there will always be wild oceans to explore."

Fiercely protective of their cultivated turf, garibaldis enliven the forests of kelp where they live with colorful personality and brilliant garb.

Sometimes called the
"Galápagos of California,"
the Channel Islands host distinctive
plants and animals,
from blue sharks to brown pelicans.
For thousands of years
the islands were home to
California's Chumash Indians.
In 1980, 1,658 square miles of
surrounding ocean were designated
as national sanctuary.

CHAPTER FOUR

A NEW WAY OF
LOOKING
AT FISH

What a delightful sensation it must be to all but
escape the eternal downpull of gravity,
to float and turn and
rise and fall at will, and all by
the least twitch of tail....

WILLIAM BEEBE
The Log of the Sun

————————————

ADRENALINE SURGED as a shadowy form passed over my head, 50 feet underwater, and disappeared into a darkening sea. Thrilled to be in the presence of a large, wild something I leaned forward hoping for another look just as the longest, widest manta ray I had ever seen loomed into view, moving as gracefully as a ballerina but weighing as much as a small elephant. This was not the first manta I had met, but it was the first I had encountered along the Kona coast of Hawaii, where thousands of people come every year to swim with these great, gentle creatures.

"Dancing with the rays," some call it. Norbert Wu, underwater photographer, describes mantas as "astonishingly docile," like "giant flying carpets" in his book of underwater experiences, *Splendors of the Sea*. Divers at the Flower Garden Banks National Marine Sanctuary always keep a lookout for these magnificent monsters, hoping for an eye-to-eye, fin-to-fin encounter. The presence of mantas in all of the nation's warm-water sanctuaries is a strong attraction for many now that the appealing nature

130

Explorer Jacques Cousteau encouraged people to dive using an Aqua-Lung, the first practical scuba, which automatically released air to the diver. He developed the system in order to "glide unhurried and unharmed, fathoms deep beneath the sea...roll over, or loll...propelled along by flippered feet," and to see fish as fish see fish—underwater.

Preceding pages: *"Suddenly, majestically, silently comes the manta," writes Greg Bunch, a researcher at Flower Garden Banks National Marine Sanctuary. "Beautiful, graceful, and serene, she pauses, somehow reaching out, inviting me to join her."*

of these giant, plankton-eating fish has been discovered. Sometimes known as "devil rays" because of their formidable size and strength, none of the several manta species has ever been recorded as attacking a person, although when speared or tangled in a net, a manta's furious reaction can pose danger to life and limb. Far from being aggressive toward swimmers or divers, mantas have become star attractions in places from Bora Bora and Hawaii to the Flower Garden Banks National Marine Sanctuary in the Gulf of Mexico. Like blue whales, they are "gentle giants," with distinctive characteristics that tempt even skeptical scientists and fishermen to murmur things about their individual behavioral quirks and "personalities." Paul Tzimoulis, for many years editor of *Skin Diver* magazine, claims, "I never met a fish I didn't like, but I harbor a special love for manta rays. Their awesome size and remarkable grace are an endless source of fascination."

We have seen that the senses and intuitions,
the various emotions and faculties…
of which man boasts may be found…
in a well-developed condition in the lower animals.

CHARLES DARWIN

We're talking about a fish here, a member of a group of some 25,000 or so aquatic species that have in common with us basic vertebrate features—two eyes, a central brain, vertebral column, heart, closed circulatory system—and much more. Instead of arms and legs they have fins, instead of fur they have scales, and they obtain oxygen not from lungs, but from their aquatic medium, gills. Many features we share with fish and some that we may not possess are developed in ways suitable for their watery realm, with resulting sensitivities we can barely conceive. Taste, for example, is not confined to a fish's mouth. Taste buds are there aplenty, but may also occur in the skin covering the lips, specialized whiskers, fins, and even the body. Feedback from taste may be vital—in combination with smell and other senses—for fish such as salmon and tuna that travel over long distances yet find their way unerringly back to very specific areas. Sensitivity to Earth's magnetic field appears to be involved with the successful travels of certain wide-ranging species. Zoologist Carl Safina observes in *Song for the Blue Ocean,* "Tuna and some other migratory fish have magnetite crystals in their brains that create a built-in compass. To our five-sense mosaic of the world, a tuna's perception is extrasensory; we cannot imagine the sensation of it."

Reactions to touch and pain appear to be exquisitely well developed in fish, as is the ability to sense minute changes of cold, heat, salinity, light, and pressure. Some fish are able to detect the weak electrical field generated by hidden prey; others use variations on the theme of chemoreception, and still others rely on acute hearing to find potential meals. Hundreds of species have electric organs capable of generating substantial shocks useful for defense, and in some cases, perhaps, for locating prey. Thousands have harnessed luminous bacteria in special organs, which serve to lure prey or distract a predator, to illuminate or communicate in an otherwise dark world.

Vision is important, of course, and in no group of animals is there greater variability of eye structure and function than among fish. The basic plan is essentially like that of all vertebrates, and most squids and octopuses: There is a transparent cornea in front of an iris, pupil, and crystalline lens; and there is a retina—the light-sensitive part of the eye. With this basic recipe, however, eyes range from specialized tubular and upward-pointing structures for certain deep-sea fish, to the large, acutely sensitive orbs of skilled predators.

Vision alone, however, is not enough. It is vital for fish to find their way and detect the presence of their fellow fish—would-be predators or would-be prey—without relying fully on sight. Among the most valuable attributes that make this possible is a pressure-sensing system, the "lateral line"—a long, fluid-filled tube with pores connected to the water outside, which runs the length of a fish's body down the middle, from the gill cover to the base of the tail.

As the fish moves through the water, slight pressure differentials are sensed by the lateral line through tiny organs that appear to function something like the semicircular canals that occur in the ears of humans. Fish do have ears, of course—although not with outward lobes that would create

FOLLOWING PAGES: *A growing network of aquariums around the nation provides splendid windows on the sea—and new ways of looking at fish and other creatures. The Monterey Bay Aquarium is dedicated to interpreting the adjacent marine sanctuary. Aquarium Executive Director Julie Packard observes: "Fifteen years and 26 million visitors since opening, it's still my conviction that we'll never run out of stories to tell about Monterey Bay."*

133

drag and otherwise interfere with typical streamlining. Hearing is, in fact, one of the most vital of senses for a fish, just as it is for marine mammals—and for us. Their inner ears are located in chambers on either side of their head, behind their eyes, much as in other vertebrates.

Notes Diane Ackerman in *A Natural History of the Senses:* "Some fish are a noisy lot. Sea robins, drum-fishes and many others make sounds with their swim bladders; croakers grunt loud enough to keep China Sea fishermen awake at night; Hawaiian triggerfish grind their teeth loudly; the male toadfish growls…. The ocean looks mute, but is alive with sounds from animals, breaking waves, tidal scouring, ship traffic, and nomadic storms, locked within the atmosphere of water as sounds are within the atmosphere of air."

Not only do many fish communicate with various croaks, thumps, groans, and grating, even high-pitched, whistling sounds, but as N. B. Marshall points out in *The Life of Fishes,* "their hearing is not inferior to that of land animals in any essential way. The ears of fish also govern orientation and balance…."

Like Wart, the young King Arthur in T. H. White's *Once and Future King,* I sometimes dream of being able to slip into the skin of a fish, to see what they see, feel what they feel. "I wish I was a fish," Wart murmured to the wizard Merlin while wistfully watching silvery shapes glide through cool water on a hot summer day. Merlin promptly obliged and turned him into a slim, swift creature with fins and scales, and for a while, Wart felt the delicious pleasure of swimming among the water weeds and getting acquainted eye to eye with snails, mussels, and other fishes. Wart "was not earthbound any more…pressed down by gravity and the weight of the atmosphere. He could do what men have always wanted to do, that is, fly…."

In the sea, anyone can fly…you can spread your arms, soar among great clouds of fish, the aquatic counterparts of birds. Hugh Downs, longtime host for ABC Television's *20/20* and a friend and diving buddy observes, "Going beneath the surface of the sea, with equipment allowing you to see and breathe, is a marvelous attitude changer. That watery realm, considered only from above, is understandably both mysterious and hostile. But in my early years of diving, I came to see it as basically friendly, and I began to feel a kinship even with the stranger forms of life there…."

Every marine sanctuary offers visitors this opportunity, by diving and snorkeling, and in Hawaii, even by passenger submarine. Most marine sanctuaries have one or more fine aquariums not far away, and even far inland, in Chicago, Chatanooga, and Albuquerque, there are increasingly popular places that now showcase underwater life in near-natural settings. Years ago, exhibits of fish tended to be like picture frames—small tanks with species selected largely for their beauty or curious nature. But many aquariums now take considerable care to replicate as nearly as possible a microcosmic view of underwater realms.

Presently, fine aquariums the world over provide windows on the world's ocean, rivers, and streams for people who otherwise would never meet grouper face to face or see the miracle of nonstop precision swimming executed by tightly packed schools of anchovy, herring, or mackerel.

The real wealth of the nation lies in the resources of the Earth—soil, water, forests, minerals, and wildlife. To utilize them for present needs while insuring their preservation for future generations requires a delicately balanced and continuing program....

RACHEL CARSON
LOST WOODS

California's Monterey Bay Aquarium is setting new standards for bringing the reality of ocean life to the public with creative displays of living kelp forests, open ocean, and even cold, dark environments. It serves as a tantalizing entrée to those who wish to explore the adjacent Monterey Bay Marine Sanctuary —whether by foot, by kayak, or by diving right in.

Long before the Monterey Bay Sanctuary came into being, divers for many years explored the nearby rocky coastline. Their voices helped bring about establishment of the Point Lobos State Reserve by the state of California. Home for 30-foot-long basking sharks, lush kelp forests, and sheer undersea cliffs and canyons, the area attracts millions of people who can visit just the upper rim of this vast ocean space directly. Many others travel vicariously to the great depths just offshore—and 10,000 feet down—via video experiences and visits with living ambassadors from the deep, in special cool, darkened chambers at the Monterey Bay Aquarium.

Executive Director Julie Packard, whose parents, David and Lucile Packard, provided the initial funding for the Aquarium and associated Monterey Bay Aquarium Research Institute, comments: "What better gift can we give the next generation than a passion for science and discovery, and a commitment to caring for the natural world?"

As a youngster, my daughter Elizabeth, who has a soft spot in her heart

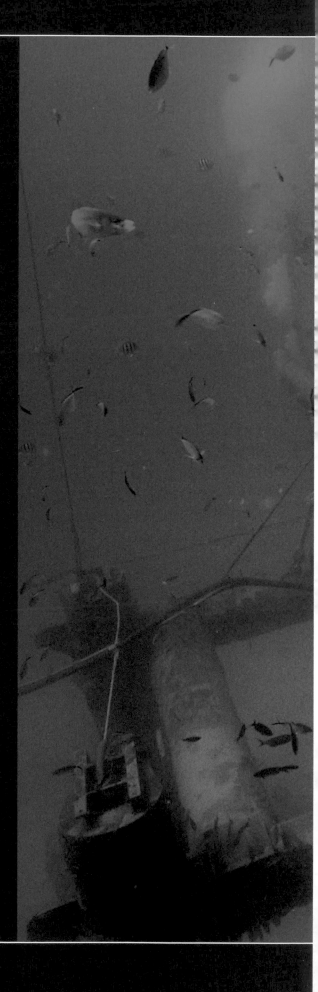

CARETAKERS

WITHIN the Florida Keys National Marine Sanctuary near Key Largo, scientists study the sea from *Aquarius,* the nation's undersea equivalent of the International Space Station. Operated by NOAA's National Underwater Research Program, the underwater laboratory provides a warm, dry home-on-the-reef. In it six aquanauts can live for up to ten days, with bunks, shower, cooking facilities, telephone, computer links—and picture windows with wondrous views of some of the nation's finest coral reefs. Pressure inside *Aquarius* keeps water from flowing in through an open hatch in the floor, making it easy for aquanauts to enter and exit at will, day or night, and thus spend six to nine hours daily away from the base, sometimes more. Sanctuary research coordinator Steve Gittings says, "Extended time makes it possible to make long-term observations of animal behavior. It also allows the animals to get used to having divers nearby, making it more likely that the observed behaviors are natural."

Aquarius, *right, the nation's underwater equivalent of the International Space Station, is located in 60 feet of water about 5 miles offshore from Key Largo, Florida. At the base of* Aquarius, *below, a school of curious resident spadefish watch author Sylvia Earle watching them.*

for all creatures, discovered as a behind-the-scenes, fish-feeding, tank-scrubbing aquarium volunteer that fish have distinctive features and even 'personalities.' "After a while, it's easy to tell one fish from another—of the same species, I mean," she said. "Anybody can see that one kind of puffer or rockfish or shark is different from another, but even if you have six bicolored damselfish together, each one is distinctive—not just by the way they look, but by the way they behave. Some are really curious, some are shy, others bold." One, a large, longtime resident grouper named Ulysses, had a reputation for being finicky, grumpy, and generally irascible, but Elizabeth eventually won his trust and he would respond to her appearance tankside with doglike enthusiasm, allowing her to do the fish equivalent for ear scratching—that is, he would lean against the side of the tank nearest to where she stood so she could happily rub the inside of his huge mouth with her small fingers and even gently massage his gills. Others who approached often got doused with an artfully aimed mouthful of saltwater laced with essence of grouper-breath.

Of all the fish in the sea, grouper are among the most appealing for divers. Jacques Cousteau, who personally speared and ate many a grouper, nonetheless wrote about them in *Silent World* with considerable affection: "The grouper is the ocean's scholar, sincerely interested in our species. It approaches us with large, touching eyes, full of puzzlement, and stays to survey us.... [Grouper] are the most inquisitive animals we have found in the sea. They sit below and look up full in our faces. With their big pectorals spread like the wings of baroque angels, they stare.... We feel sure that we could tame one, by training that generous curiosity, toward becoming a pet."

Bob Wicklund, pioneering diver and biologist, has spent many years studying Nassau grouper in the Florida Keys Sanctuary and elsewhere, and is impressed with their knack for problem solving. For a research project on the effectiveness of fish traps, a chunk of bait was placed inside a small wire cage and checked frequently to see who might have been lured inside. Wicklund approached the cage once, just as a large Nassau grouper began nosing around the entrance to the trap. "The opening was simply too small for the grouper to squeeze through, so it began swimming slowly around the cage, eyeing the bait," he said. "After several minutes of apparent frustration, the fish moved to one side of the cage, flipped over on its side and began swishing its big tail up and down, which caused the bait to flow to the far side. The grouper then swam over and bit off a chunk that protruded through the mesh. I watched as the fish did this over and over, until most of the bait was gone."

I first began to recognize fish as individuals and look at them in new ways in 1970, when I spent two weeks as a resident in a special ocean laboratory parked on a coral reef 50 feet underwater. Using the gift of extended time, I set out to watch the behavior of the local residents — the fish. What I did not expect, however, was that the fish also would do a lot of watching. Many seemed as curious about me as I was about them.

Who knows what admirable virtue of fishes may be
below the low-water mark,
bearing up against a hard destiny,
not admired by that fellow creature who alone
can appreciate it! Who hears the fishes when they cry?
It will not be forgotten by some memory that
we were contemporaries.

HENRY DAVID THOREAU

Before dawn, my dive partners and I would roll out of our warm, dry bunks; pull on lightweight, foam-rubber wet suits; strap on scuba tanks or special silent rebreathing systems, masks, and fins; pick up cameras, notepads and other equipment; then step through a round hatch in the floor and glide into the ocean beyond. In some ways, it was like going to the aquarium — inside out, with us on display for the fish. In the hours before sunrise, we swam without dive-lights, reveling instead in luminescence generated by small, glowing creatures that sparkled like stars as we moved among them. As darkness faded, there was a distinct surge of activity as sleeping fish — parrotfish, filefish, angelfish, wrasses, butterfly fish, and other day-active creatures — emerged from crevices and crannies and set out to make their rounds on the reef. Some of the nocturnal fish — cardinal fish, squirrel fish, and beautiful redfish known as "big eyes" — moved into the shadowed spaces just vacated.

I got to know five gray angelfish rather well because every dawn they would appear in loose formation on the same section of reef and follow me around for awhile, as if they were really interested in what I was doing. During those dawn rendezvous I began to see each as a distinctive being — as unique as a cat, dog, or horse. The smallest tended to lag behind the others. The largest was set apart by size and also by a white patch around its mouth. Each had markings as subtle and individual as fingerprints. *(continued on page 147)*

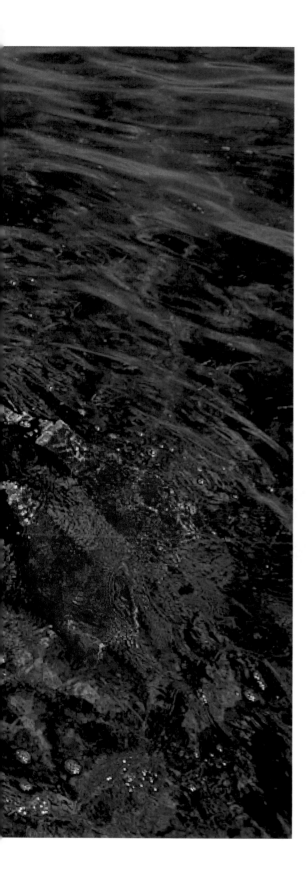

With face mask, fins, and a snorkel, almost anyone can
feel the joy of weightlessness and meet wild sea creatures as curious about you
as you are about them, as these visitors, at left, are doing in the
Florida Keys National Marine Sanctuary.

Other ways to watch fish in action—and to vicariously enjoy
their aquatic space—are through passenger submarines and glass-bottom
boats, such as the one above, which enable visitors to
dive dry while admiring the sea life below.

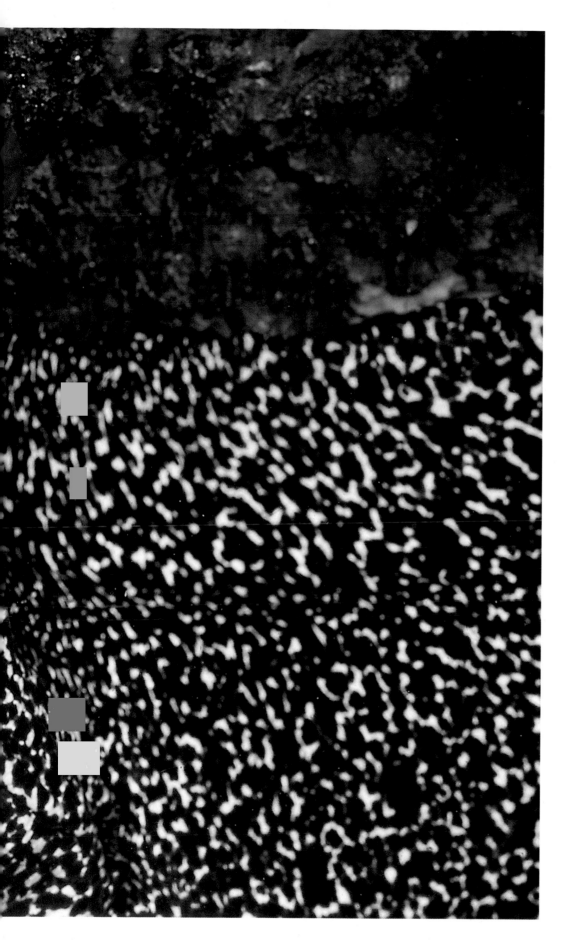

A fearsome face full of sharp teeth
belies the basically gentle nature
of the moray eel. An octopus or small
fish could be in trouble
when nose to nose with one,
but divers have little to fear around
this spotted beauty. To find it, look in
crevices 60 feet underwater,
about 100 miles south of Galveston,
Texas, near the Flower Garden Banks
National Marine Sanctuary.

Sir Peter Scott, artist and famed founder of the World Wildlife Fund, once showed me his rogues' gallery of swans—hundreds of individual portraits that he and Philippa, his wife, had assembled over years of observing and documenting wild birds who came to his front yard at Slimbridge, England. "When we noticed that the base of the bill for every swan is configured in a unique pattern, we started to give each one a name," he explained. "Getting to know them as individuals helps us understand their interactions, as well as basic information about where they go. It's as effective as a bird band[ing], but it comes naturally."

The Scotts readily made the connection between birds and fish when they both became avid scuba divers. Peter Scott often took materials to draw and paint his subjects, on the spot, even underwater. For hours, he would sit and allow the fish to gather as he sketched. "Sometimes I have to shoo them away so I can work," he said, "and once, a particularly persistent parrotfish kept trying to bite the bright lines I was making with crayons right off the page."

Recently, while living 60 feet underwater for a week in the nation's newest underwater laboratory, *Aquarius,* in the Florida Keys National Marine Sanctuary near Key Largo, my teammates and I got to know many of the local residents personally. "Lurch," a great silver barracuda, hovered just outside the bunkroom window, drawn to small fish attracted to the lab's lights—but also taking in the view of the resting primates within. Five large tarpon, each readily identifiable as an individual, often swam around the lab, and sometimes sailed by us at high speed like a squadron of sleek aircraft when we cruised along the reef. Every day we looked for a certain nurse shark who often parked under a ledge about a thousand feet away from *Aquarius,* and we also checked to see if we could find the two red grouper and giant green moray who lived nearby.

Billy Causey, superintendent of the Florida Keys Sanctuary, pointed out a large coral head and cluster of sponges inhabited by eight fist-size

Among the most curious, good-natured fish in the sea,
Nassau grouper cannot stand not knowing what's going on. Sometimes called
"Labrador retrievers of the sea," these once common residents of Florida reefs
are now rare and fully protected there. In her Book of Fishes,
Hillary Hauser suggests one of the reasons why the grouper is vulnerable:
"Its friendly and inquisitive nature makes it an easy target."

butterflyfish. They flowed like dabs of sunlight, first dancing as one, then moving apart, then again turning in unison, as if responding to secret music. They were there every day when we swam by, and at night we found them tucked in nearby crevices. "Many butterflyfish mate for life and live for years," Billy reminded me. "They're so beautiful, people often capture them for home aquariums, but taking them disrupts close-knit social structures—and alters the nature of the reef itself." By visiting the "big aquarium"—the ocean itself—anyone can enjoy getting to know these.

We can no longer think of our oceans as infinite, or
its resources as boundless. We have opened a new chapter in conservation history,
akin to a century ago when we settled the continent.
Yet recognizing limits—first on land, now at sea—is not a question of
closing frontiers, but of opening them."

BRUCE BABBITT
SECRETARY OF THE INTERIOR

Our fellow aquanauts—Steve Gittings, of the National Marine Sanctuary's research program, and geologist Ellen Prager—teamed up to redocument stations that Steve had helped set up several years before near *Aquarius.* They found the old markers and re-established transect lines; then, using video and still cameras, they swam along the previously filmed pathways. By going to the same places repeatedly over time, and counting the number, kind, and condition of corals, sponges, algae, urchins, lobsters, fish, and other reef residents, it is possible to help gauge trends—and maybe understand underlying problems of reef decline. Since the 1960s, when many scientists first began observing coral reefs and assessing their health, there has been significant deterioration worldwide. Knowledge gained by long-term studies of coral reefs in marine sanctuaries—the Florida Keys, Flower Garden Banks, and Fagatele Bay—is especially valuable as a baseline to help evaluate impacts from fishing, pollution, and other human actions. Annually thousands of volunteers working with the Center for Marine Conservation and Ted Danson's American Oceans Campaign help clean up the beaches and the underwater reefs in many of the sanctuaries.

And more recently, establishing monitoring stations is an important objective of the National Marine Sanctuaries Program in conjunction with the National Geographic's Sustainable Seas Expeditions. This involves taking regular inventories of the fish. Fish populations are typically estimated by dragging a net through the sea and extrapolating the number that are in a certain area, based on how many are caught. "Catch per unit effort" is a favored method that draws on data gathered by boats using similar gear for known periods of time. Sometimes population estimates are inferred from the number of fish tagged, released, and subsequently caught.

Bottom trawls, however, damage and disrupt the structure and communities of life on the seafloor, and in all cases many creatures—from turtles and birds to crabs and jellyfish—are unintentionally caught and killed in the process of trying to capture targeted fish species. Better techniques are being explored: Acoustic devices developed to find and track enemy submarines are now being applied to determine the presence and abundance of creatures hundreds or thousands of feet away. But a new method promises to significantly refine the way fish populations are evaluated— one that is kind to the critters and yields far more information than just number and size of a few species.

National Marine Sanctuaries extend the conservation ethic to
the sea and expand it to include sustainable development.
We are creating management plans for the sanctuaries that balance conservation
and commerce. These sanctuaries will ensure that we nurture
the sea and the wonderful creatures that live in it so that future generations
will have them to explore and enjoy.

WILLIAM DALEY
SECRETARY OF COMMERCE

Based on the century-old methods developed by the Audubon Society and others to census birds, the "Great American Fish Count" was launched in 1992 in the Channel Islands National Marine Sanctuary and Channel Islands National Park to begin to evaluate the status of fish directly. Since then, formal fish-watching has won thousands of followers who not only have fun getting to know the fish, but also help with the scientific assessment of the state of the sanctuaries.

The American Oceans Campaign, based in California, and the Reef Environmental Education Foundation (REEF), in Florida, as well as NOAA, enlist snorkelers and divers to participate in counts in many marine sanctuaries. All that is required is a willingness to get acquainted with who's who among the fish in the area being sampled, to *(continued on page 154)*

COUNTING COUNTS

SINCE 1992, starting in the Channel Islands National Park and National Marine Sanctuary, snorkelers and divers have been following the example set by bird-watchers for the past century: conducting formal fish counts, with disciplined protocols, seminars for fish-watching techniques, checklists, and follow-up meetings to compare discoveries.

Thousands around the nation now participate in the annual "Great American Fish Count,"

held in July and August in many of the marine sanctuaries; and some counters continue to take notes on how many of what kinds of fish and other marine creatures they see on dives all year-round. Those interested in filling out a life list of the species they observe have plenty of excuses to travel widely and to dive often: about 25,000 species are known and about a hundred new species are discovered every year.

Information gathered is

valuable for the growing program of research and long-term monitoring at locations throughout the sanctuary system. The method provides a welcome, non-obtrusive alternative to traditional fish-census techniques. As part of the National Geographic's Sustainable Seas Expeditions, fish-counting surveys from the *Deep Worker* submersible are being used in marine sanctuaries for the first time, in depths to 2,000 feet.

Grunts, Florida Keys

A snorkeler, opposite, takes notes on an underwater slate during a fish count in the Florida Keys Sanctuary. Above, schooling grunts manage to maintain position without bumping into one another, thanks to pressure-sensitive organs in a gill-to-tail lateral line. Like many fish, grunts vocalize—hence, their name.

Irish Lord, Channel Islands

LET'S FACE IT

This collection of mug shots is but a sample of the enormous diversity of fish species in the nation's marine sanctuaries: Upper left, an elegant Irish Lord courses the Channel Islands; lower left, a pair of lizardfish sport distinctive paisley patterns; below, a well-named porcupine fish peers from its armor; and a wolf eel probes with a pillowy lip, protection against the spiny urchins it eats. Above right, two California sheepsheads communicate, mouth to mouth; and below right, a jewel-like eye peers from the face of a fist-size frogfish.

Porcupine Fish, Florida Keys

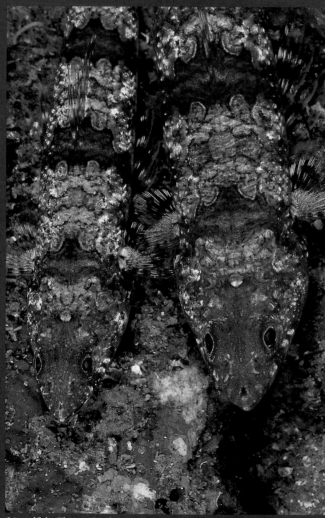

Lizardfish, Flower Garden Banks

Wolf Eel, Olympic Coast

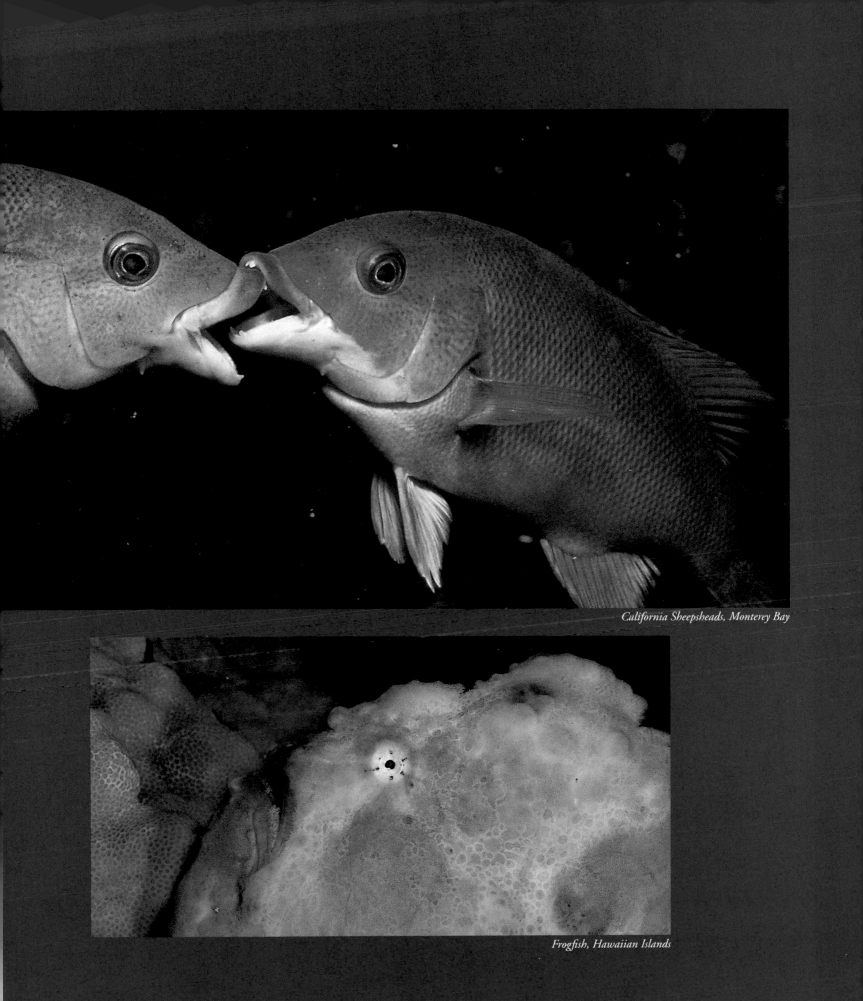

California Sheepsheads, Monterey Bay

Frogfish, Hawaiian Islands

follow certain protocols for estimating numbers, to jump in with an underwater slate and survey forms, then keep track of what you see. Special seminars are held and guidebooks are available for those who want to brush up on the subtle differences among the dozens of species commonly encountered, and to get direction about unusual things to look for. Useful information can be gathered anytime, anywhere, by almost anyone, but most popular are annual events comparable to Christmas bird counts, where thousands of people gather—from Gray's Reef in the Atlantic, to the Florida Keys and the Flower Garden Banks in the Gulf of Mexico, to California's coast—to concurrently take the plunge and bring back news of what they find. The Sustainable Seas Expeditions will now be heavily involved in the fish counts, and with use of the *DeepWorker* submersibles as well as small, remotely operated vehicles, census-taking may reach new depths of 2,000 feet.

As more and more people become involved in fish counts, fish-watching for science, or just enjoying the presence of fish as a part of what makes the ocean appealing, the value of these amazingly diverse creatures to humankind begins to take on new meaning. But at the same time that we have begun to appreciate their value to us as fish alive, we are also facing a troubling reality: the swift, sharp decline of many once abundant species.

The problems are many, including years of overfishing and destructive catch techniques that are undermining the stability of fish populations and the nature of the vital systems from which they are being taken.

In many ways fish are to the sea as wild birds and mammals are to the land: Many are edible, and in the early part of the century, many birds and mammals in North America were taken in huge numbers for commercial markets. Like fish, some species such as buffalo were swiftly reduced to perilously low numbers or, like passenger pigeons, were pushed to extinction. Such a fate may be avoided for cod, haddock, shark, bluefin tuna, salmon, and other exploited species if actions are taken before it is too late. This requires an understanding of how to protect fish in the sea, just as it does for wildlife on the land.

Many who want to hunt quail, turkey, duck, or geese recognize that for these creatures to prosper, it is necessary to protect their feeding and breeding areas; most agree that it is reasonable that such wildlife be hunted only in some places and only at certain times, with constraints on size, number, and kind that can be removed. Burning forests or grasslands to concentrate wildlife for easier capture is no longer condoned, nor is it legal to use bull-dozers or other destructive techniques to gather birds or land mammals.

In the ocean there are few constraints on taking wildlife. Even though most fishing within the nation's Exclusive Economic Zone does comply with the law, it is still legal to use trawls or dredges that scrape the seafloor and do damage to habitats and animals while obtaining fish, shrimp, or other commercially valuable species. In addition, only a fraction of one percent of the nation's waters have been designated as places where fish and other marine life are completely free of predation by us—even within the national marine sanctuaries. This may change.

In 1996, Congress passed legislation aimed at protecting and restoring the nation's depleted oceans. Known as the Magnuson-Stevens Act, it notes: "One of the greatest long-term threats to the viability of commercial and recreational fisheries is the continuing loss of marine, estuarine, and other aquatic habitats. Habitat considerations should receive increased attention for the conservation and management of fishery resources of the U.S." The act has stimulated new interest in protected areas in the sea, including the value of marine sanctuaries.

Not only do sanctuaries afford full protection in special "no take" zones—as limited as they may be, they also provide people the close and vital contact needed for developing a rapport with fish alive. It also prepares us to face the next concern: that protection for fish in the sea must start at the headwaters of rivers and the tops of mountains.

American eels may be able to survive years in the wild ocean as planktonic larvae after hatching near the Sargasso Sea, but be doomed when they migrate to the rivers and streams of their ancestors, where they may be captured in nets or run into dams that block access to their traditional streams—or encounter toxins that kill them outright.

Atlantic salmon and various Pacific varieties—silver, king, coho, chinook, sockeye, steelhead, chum, pink—survive the perils of life in the open sea, only to cope with increasingly formidable barriers in the rivers they must swim to return to their spawning grounds.

Writer and photographer Natalie Fobes in her moving book about salmon, *Reaching Home,* observes: "[we have] the outdated and erroneous idea that we as individuals cannot harm a species as great as the Pacific salmon. We can. And we have. At stake is an intricate network of interdependencies ranging from the prosperity of microorganisms in the mountain streams when young salmon hatch, to the needs of bears, eagles, and other terrestrial species that ... rely on spawning salmon for ... sustenance."

Along the Olympic coast, herculean efforts are under way to help salmon. Not only is there a limit on the number of adults taken at sea, but also adults are aided in safe transportation upstream to spawning grounds, and young on their way to the sea are helped downstream past dams, turbines, mining operations, polluted waters, and other obstacles.

In the salmon we recognize a miraculous natural phenomenon—one example of millions of others that occur with every creature in the sea. We see how vital it is to protect what remains of the systems that were already ancient long before the first human footprint marked the Earth.

In a reflective moment, Natalie Fobes described salmon as "a sea-bright shuttle weaving the rain-green world of the temperate Pacific watersheds." Perhaps no creature on Earth better symbolizes life as a tapestry of individual but interconnecting threads between land and sea and between salmon and the rest of the living world. Each single thread touches hundreds of others; each one lost or weakened diminishes all.

Often I have reflected about the human future and life in the sea with writer, poet, and sage Reeve Lindbergh, and recently asked her to comment on how the ocean and its creatures touch all of us. In her response there is a ring of hope for the "sea-bright" salmon, the mysterious eels, the curious grouper, the skeins of silver fish, the seabirds, great forests, the future of humankind—and Earth itself:

"The history of the planet has always been a unity: Earth, sea, and sky, and all created things evolving together, generation after generation. This remains true. If the integrity of the sea is threatened, then Earth and sky are also compromised, and so are we ourselves, and our children. To protect the oceans, where life was born, is to begin an active understanding that it is only through our commitment to the unity of life on Earth that life can continue for us all."

Largest fish in the ocean, whale sharks occur in tropical seas worldwide, including the nation's marine sanctuaries in the Florida Keys, the northern Gulf of Mexico, Hawaii, and American Samoa. Photographer David Doubilet described an encounter with a 50-foot long beauty whose "...mouth was like a gigantic Hoover, a Hoover from Mars.... Spotting me, she turned away with delicate, elephantine grace."

Millions of tons of fish, and other creatures, are taken from
the sea every year by commercial fishermen such as those
above. Diminishing returns for U.S. fishermen in recent times
led to legislation in 1996, known as the Magnuson-Stevens
Act, to help conserve what remains of once numerous species.
The act includes protection of critical habitats for fish.

Great schools of small anchovies, right, as well as herring,
capelin, and other small, schooling species of fish are
vital links in complex ocean systems. Their decline means
hard times for seabirds, whales, seals, sea lions
and many kinds of fish, from cod and haddock to high-seas
swordfish, marlin, and tuna.

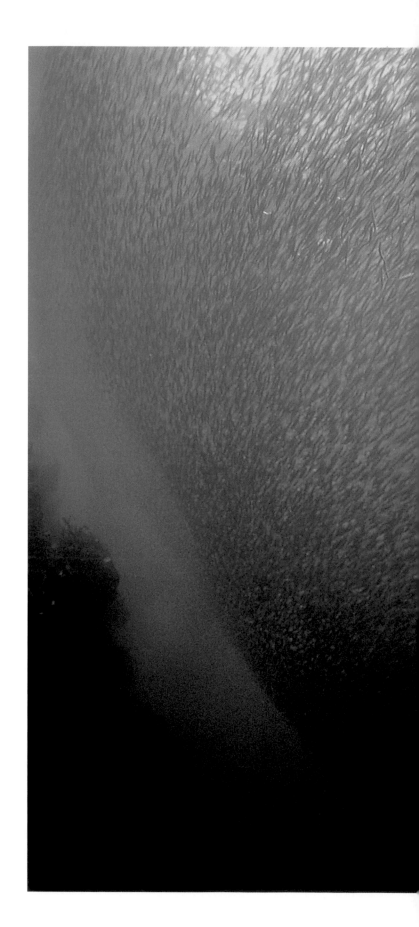

FOLLOWING PAGES: *A biplane ride gives a seabird's-eye view of reefs in the Florida Keys Sanctuary. About 2 percent of the 3,700 square miles of reefs are fully protected—called "no take" areas.*

Gentle and curious,
ocean sunfish are vulnerable targets
for underwater photographers—
as well as for sea lions,
who often tug on their fins
during playful encounters in
the Channel Islands
National Marine Sanctuary.
Often called "swimming heads,"
sunfish translate their diet of
jellyfish into bodies of giant
proportion, weighing several
hundred pounds.

CHAPTER FIVE

THE SWEEP OF TIME

What is this sea, and wherein lies its power so greatly to stir the minds of men?
What is the mystery of it, intangible, yet inseparably its own?
Perhaps part of the mystery resides in its hoary antiquity, for the sea is almost as old as
earthly time.... For hundreds of millions of years, all life was sealife,
developing in prodigious abundance and variety...."

RACHEL CARSON
LOST WOODS

WITHIN THE WILD OCEAN, in places designated as national marine sanctuaries, deep history awaits—in coastal marshes, along the rocky shorelines, within submarine canyons, in the richly fragrant muds and sloping mounds of sand, along sunlit meadows of seagrass and the sheltering branches of coral on a reef—wherever there is life. The distillation of all preceding time is there, reflected in lacy strands of sponges, in the diaphanous tissues of jellyfish, the delicate flash of color in a passing squid, the knobby hide of a starfish—all little changed in basic design in hundreds of millions of years. From microscopic marine life to the largest living creature ever, there await mysteries, secrets—and solutions, perhaps, to some of humankind's most vexing questions.

How did life begin? Where did we come from? Where might we be going? How are we going to get to wherever that is? How can we find an enduring place for ourselves within the natural systems that sustain us? What can we learn from the past that will help guide us in the future? In these special protected areas bordering our shores, much awaits discovery concerning our own geologically recent history, stored in thousands of

Face to face with ancient history, a diver near Monterey, California,
greets a giant jellyfish—a creature whose relatives preceded
dinosaurs by hundreds of millions of years.

PRECEDING PAGES: *Awash in mist that for centuries has bathed its
Pacific shores, Point Sur, near the Monterey Bay Marine Sanctuary, yields
the faint glow of a 19th-century lighthouse.*

shipwrecks, in fragments of pottery, etchings on rock—and in the lives of people whose culture existed in a time long before Columbus steered a course to this continent.

My parents often entertained my brothers and me with stories about how the world was when they were young, before cars and airplanes and radios, before television, computer games, and satellites circling the Earth. With them, I dreamed about what it must have been like during the time of their grandparents, when great herds of buffalo and antelope grazed western prairies and enormous flocks of passenger pigeons, shorebirds, and waterfowl darkened the skies along the eastern seaboard in spring and fall. Sometimes I plunged deeper still in time, imagining North America when present cities and farms were home to woolly mammoths, saber-toothed cats, and giant sloths, or even a hundred million years ago, when dinosaurs prowled fern-filled forests and dragonflies the size of eagles swooped low over lakes and marshes. What must it have been like, I wonder still, before animals existed at all, billions of years ago—when all life was microbial and entirely marine?

Arriving on this planet as it was three billion years ago, or even two billion, could be as dangerous for us as setting foot on Mars today with no space suit. There was then on Earth plenty of water and, for food, numerous nutritious microorganisms, but not enough oxygen in the atmosphere to support life as we know it, let alone the amazingly stable mix we now enjoy— 21 percent oxygen, 79 percent nitrogen plus smidgens of other gases such as .13 percent carbon dioxide. It took a long time before microbes mastered the magic of photosynthesis, and ages longer for organisms to produce more than was consumed, arriving, eventually at the state that we now take for granted as "normal." Today the atmosphere on Mars is 95 percent carbon dioxide, for Venus, 98 percent. Sidney Liebes notes in *A Walk Through Time,* "It took Earth's life-forms billions of years to pump the carbon dioxide from our atmosphere and transform it into oil deposits while filling the atmosphere with nitrogen and the oxygen we need to breathe."

To help imagine the magnitude of time it has taken to get to where we are now, geologist Don Eicher in his book *Geologic Time* suggests thinking of the 4.6 billion years since the birth of our solar system as a single year. Begin in January. Months pass before the appearance of life in the sea—in May; not until sometime in November does terrestrial life begin; and it takes until mid-December before there are dinosaurs. They disappear on the 26th, at about the same time the Rocky Mountains are uplifted. Our distant human ancestors show up sometime during the evening of the 31st of December, and the most recent ice age recedes from the Great Lakes and Northern Europe just before midnight on the 31st, marking the beginning of an exceptionally congenial 10,000-year era of benign warmth and the beginning of major developments in human civilization—agriculture, writing, permanent cities, and much more. Columbus discovers America just three seconds before midnight.

Like a bit of plankton, I have drifted in a small, translucent submarine deep into the modern seas bordering North America, and wondered what it would be like to have been there in November of Eicher's year of compressed time. The supercontinent referred to by geologists as Pangaea had begun to break apart, and the chunk that would become North America was easing into existence. Little would look familiar on the land 600 million years ago—no leafy flowering plants, not even mosses to soften the shorelines of ponds or angular rock surfaces; underwater, then as now, there would be jellyfish, their fragile-looking appearance belying a durable recipe for survival through hundreds of millions of years of change.

Myriad sea creatures find refuge in the Monitor's *bent and broken*
body now cloaked in corals, sponges, sea fans, and anemones. It takes
but a moment in time for an object of our making to become
part of the eternal sea.

JOHN D. BROADWATER
MANAGER, MONITOR *MARINE SANCTUARY*

As a seven-year-old, biologist Edward O. Wilson recalls staring down at a huge jellyfish in shallow water along a Florida beach: "The creature is astonishing. It existed outside my previous imagination.... Its opalescent pink bell is divided by thin red lines that radiate from center to circular ridge. A wall of tentacles falls from the rim to surround and partially veil a feeding tube and other organs, which fold in and out like the fabric of a drawn curtain.... It came into my world abruptly, from I knew not where...."

FOLLOWING PAGES: *Regarded by some as the "perfect fish," bluefin tuna*
migrate over thousands of miles, sometimes traveling as fast as a nuclear submarine.
Fine-tuned over millions of years for survival in the open sea, these swift,
sleek masters of the ocean sometimes cooperate to capture their prey.

To see such a creature is to glimpse a time traveler of sorts, a fragment of living history, a window onto Earth's adolescence, a living ambassador from an era that today exists only in dreams.

It took until about half a billion years ago for sufficient oxygen to accumulate in Earth's atmosphere to power more than microscopic creatures, whereupon major divisions of life swiftly developed that are still evident today. You can encounter much of this diversity on a mudflat, in a kelp forest, or suspended midwater in the living liquid broth that makes up most of the ocean, including many divisions of animals that have no representatives in fresh water or on land at all. Those that were most successful in the transition from sea to shore and beyond managed to capture the essence of saltwater within a shell or protective gelatinous sheath or cell wall. We ourselves begin life in a captive ocean of fluid, and upon birth, must successfully make the transition to air while maintaining within our own veins and arteries a saline fluid hauntingly like that of the sea. No matter where on Earth we live, we are constantly reminded of our need to replenish the water essential for our immediate survival and well-being—and water needed for the prosperity of the organisms we rely on for our sustenance.

Early on, insects, spiders, centipedes, and other terrestrial arthropods mastered the trick of taking water with them when they left the sea, a strategy made possible because of their flexible exoskeleton surrounding a saline interior —a critical breakthrough in body design that enabled this division of life to become ultimately the most diverse of all animals, in and out of the sea.

One arthropod that has mastered both realms is the horseshoe crab, a large, craggy-looking relict from a time long before there were fish in the sea. It's easy to find them in the Florida Keys National Marine Sanctuary during the summer, plowing into soft sand or swimming upside down just under the water's surface, looking rather like a glossy brown salad bowl with lots of legs, several eyes, and a spiky tail. As a child I was fascinated by the hundreds that came ashore on New Jersey beaches, and I never tired of picking them up and trying to get them to go back into the sea where I knew they belonged. Later,

Little changed in 350 million years, horseshoe crabs are durable— but vulnerable—envoys from the distant past. More closely related to spiders and scorpions than to crabs and shrimp, these once numerous "living fossils" face an uncertain future because of habitat loss and use of large numbers of egg-bearing females for eel bait by fishermen.

I discovered that they wanted to be high on the beach because that's where the females needed to lay their eggs, and the males naturally followed close behind—sometimes actually hitching a ride by grasping the shell of a willing mother-to-be and being pulled along.

In times past, some horseshoe crabs apparently made it ashore permanently as forest residents in the same way, perhaps, that pill bugs have abandoned their salty origins to inhabit backyard gardens and woodlands— crustaceans far from the sea. Similarly, earthworms and leeches are derived from distant ocean ancestors with a wanderlust, although the sea has remained home to the great majority of their annelid relatives. More closely related to spiders and scorpions than to crabs, horseshoe crabs have survived massive changes that extinguished many of their contemporaries from hundreds of millions of years ago. Four species now exist, three in Asian waters, and one, *Limulus polyphemus,* that has somehow found a place for itself along the Atlantic seaboard from Maine to the Yucatán peninsula.

Once so common that people in the northeastern United States gathered these amazing "living fossils" for road-building materials, fertilizer, and fence construction, horseshoe crabs are in sharp decline, partly because of past exploitation, but also because truckloads are taken now for use as eel bait by fishermen. Even more critical may be the loss of the suitable areas needed for successful nesting—and places for the young to grow for the eight or nine years needed to mature. The marine sanctuaries we have established can help them, and in some unexpected ways, the horseshoe crabs can—and do—help us.

Copper compounds in the blood of horseshoe crabs have proven useful in certain medical tests, and their ten primitive eyes have proven extraordinarily helpful in understanding how our own visual systems work. Many value the crabs primarily because certain migrating shorebirds have come to depend on horseshoe crab eggs as a vital source of food during the birds' long migration from the tip of South America to northern Canada. But for some of us, it's enough to know that here is a survivor, a special rare and wonderful link to our deep past, worthy of respect and care if for no reason other than because living fossils, perhaps, should be given a chance to live on.

Hugh Downs acknowledges our link to horseshoe crabs and all creatures of the past: "we are our brothers' keepers. For purely expedient reasons we must protect that life since without it we would die. But there is a deeper reason for caring. All of them down there are our flesh and blood."

Looking at fossils etched in rocks, there are many tantalizing clues about the kinds of creatures that once swam in ancient seas, and of those that left life's cradle and ventured onto land. John "Jack" Horner, dedicated dinosaur expert, in *Dinosaur Lives* says that when he began looking for fossils years ago, he was "motivated by nothing more than the desire to witness something I hadn't seen before—to be surprised—which, come to think of it, is the same thing that motivates me today." Explorations of the past century have yielded many surprises, not only about wondrous creatures now extinct, but also about ancient forms of life that still abound.

We are apt to look out on the great ocean and regard it as but a half-blank
part of our globe—a sort of desert, a "waste of water." But we may
at length discover that the sea is as full of life as the land.

JOHN MUIR
THOUSAND MILE WALK TO THE GULF

One such event was the discovery in the sea in 1977 of places where super-heated water spurts from deep within the Earth through hydrothermal vents, giving rise to rich mineral deposits and entire communities of life unlike anything previously known. Far from the faintest glimmer of solar radiance, bacteria prosper, deriving energy not from sunlight transformed through photosynthesis, but by chemosynthesis, a process that provides clues about how life began—and continues still—in ways that we are just beginning to grasp. Along with the bacteria, certain microbes thrived that appeared distinctively different, but it took 20 years of careful research, including genome analysis, for scientists to conclude that a new kingdom of life, the *Archaea*, needed to be named in recognition of the extraordinary nature of its life-forms.

Finding new species is easy to do, especially in the deep ocean where so much remains to be explored. According to Fred Grassle, one of the first scientists to study life associated with hydrothermal vents, more than 20 new families or subfamilies, 50 new genera, and over 100 new species have been identified from these small areas alone, as well as the new kingdom mentioned above. About a million-and-a-half species have been named and described by scientists since the process of formally dignifying creatures with scientific epithets began in the mid-1700s, but the number of unnamed species is estimated to be from ten to a hundred million, maybe more. Only about 10 percent of the species that are believed to occur on coral reefs have been described so far, and an even smaller percentage is accounted for from deep-sea environments. The Sustainable Seas Expeditions will be on the *(continued on page 184)*

Land and sea converge,
and so does the ethic of caring
along Washington's Olympic coast.
Olympic National Park
oversees about 60 miles of shoreline,
complemented by the 3,310-square-mile
Olympic Coast National Marine
Sanctuary, which extends along the
shore and out to sea, from
Cape Flattery to the mouth of
the Copalis River.

EARLY LIFE

IN AN AREA you can encircle with your arms there may be more broad divisions of life—on a coral reef, in a kelp forest, on a rocky shore, or in a mudflat—than on any comparable land area. Nearly all the major categories of plants and animals have some representation in the sea; only half occur in terrestrial or freshwater environments. Most have ancient origins, from minute protozoans and diverse sponges, jellies, sea stars, and worms to sophisticated mollusks and crustacea. A Christmas-tree worm is related to the earthworm; a Spanish-shawl nudibranch is a snail without a shell.

Christmas-tree worm, Flower Garden Banks

Spanish-shawl nudibranch and crimson anemone, Channel Islands

A living tapestry of sea stars, sponges, and nudibranchs adorns a rocky overhang, Monterey Bay.

EARLY LIFE

With a beguiling crown of tentacles, a sea anemone invites passing fish and small crustacea to investigate; some stay—to become a meal for the anemone. Relatives of corals, jellyfish, and sea pens, anemones are thought to be among the earliest forms of multicellular life.

Anemone, near Olympic Coast Marine Sanctuary

EARLY LIFE

Crustacea are to the sea what insects are to the land—diverse arthropod "middlemen" who translate energy from the small creatures they dine upon into an amazingly diverse array of body forms and lifestyles. In turn, they are consumed by numerous other creatures in a sea's eat-and-be-eaten crucible of life. The squid and the octopus, the most intelligent of all invertebrates, are vital to the survival of certain seals, sea lions, seabirds, dolphins, whales, and many kinds of fish. Some occur in vast numbers, others are extremely rare, but all have a value to us scientifically, economically, and aesthetically, that transcends their worth as a commodity.

Hermit crab, Fagatele Bay

*A hermit crab, above, peers from an adopted shell at
Fagatele Bay, in American Samoa. Like a living jewel, a small squid,
opposite, darts through a black sea.*

Squid, Channel Islands

lookout for new species as researchers explore in *DeepWorker* submersibles.

Any day now, I expect to see headlines announcing that someone has at last met up with the squid of all squids, *Architeuthis dux,* or giant squid, known only from pieces washed ashore or found in the stomachs of sperm whales. No one has seen one alive, underwater. In his recent fictional epic, *Beast,* Peter Benchley writes about a giant quid who has acquired a taste for small submersibles with scientists inside, an unlikely scenario, but one that those of us who pilot *DeepWorker* submersibles will have in mind, especially while exploring the canyons within the Monterey Bay and Channel Islands National Marine Sanctuaries, and other deep waters worldwide, where giant squids are known to occur.

Something about squids and their eight-armed cousins, the octopuses, brings out almost entirely unwarranted visions of monsters intent on consuming us. Years ago, when Thor Heyerdahl crossed the Pacific Ocean on a balsa wood raft, *Kon Tiki,* he said, "The National Geographic Society had shown us reports and dramatic magnesium photographs from an area in the Humboldt Current where monstrous octopuses had their favorite resort and came up on the surface at night.... They had arms which could make an end of a big shark and set ugly marks on great whales.... We were reminded that they lay floating in the darkness with phosphorescent eyes.... We did not at all like the prospect of feeling cold arms round our necks, dragging us out of our sleeping bags at night, and we provided ourselves with saber-like machete knives, one for each of us, in case we should wake to the embrace of fumbling tentacles."

Heyerdahl and his crew never learned what it was like to be awakened by the embrace of a slippery-armed cephalopod, and no one yet knows what a giant squid will do in the presence of a small submarine, yet every octopus and squid I have ever known (and I have met more than a few) has been charmingly gentle, curious, and typically, rather shy.

Douglas Chadwick and Joel Sartore observe in *The Company We Keep:* "Most wildlife is small; the average length for animal species is well under half an inch.... The very existence of most big life-forms rests upon legions of smaller ones." Yet, not all newly discovered organisms are tiny. About two new species of birds are found every year, and approximately a hundred new kinds of fish. In 1976, the megamouth shark, a gray-brown beauty with bioluminescent lips, was recovered from deep water near Hawaii, and later, along the coast of California. As recently as 1991, a previously unknown kind of beaked whale was found; and in 1990, a new primate was discovered living on a small island just offshore from São Paulo, Brazil.

Occasionally a new phylum turns up, as was the case in the early 1990s when a tiny but distinctly different bit of life was discovered prospering among the whiskers of North Atlantic lobsters, and in 1983, when a previously unknown phylum was found living among sand grains in the ocean in depths from 30 to 1,500 feet deep. Discovering something that ranks as a new phylum is big news. After all, all fish, amphibians, reptiles, birds, mammals, and some small and less well-known creatures who live in the ocean are generally assembled together in one phylum, the *Chordata*. Given that within the past 20 years thousands of new species, new phyla, and a kingdom of life have been designated, it makes one wonder what else is out there, down there, awaiting discovery.

Another compelling reason underlying the concept of marine sanctuaries relates to the need to protect biodiversity—both the creatures we know, as well as the largely unexplored treasury of life we have not yet met. All are at risk. In *Biodiversity II,* biologist Marjorie Reaka-Kudla says, "Undocumented diversity and—of particular importance at the present time—undocumented contemporary extinctions—are likely to be higher than we realize in marine environments." A great many marine creatures have a small range, and therefore are vulnerable to loss when shorelines are altered, destructive fishing techniques are used, or other habitat losses occur.

It's amazing what you find in your own backyard.
Just a few miles off the coast of southern California a new species
had been discovered that was completely unknown to science.
For more than a week the waters were filled with them. Then one morning,
as mysteriously as they appeared,
the jellyfish vanished and have never been seen again.

HOWARD HALL
SECRETS OF THE OCEAN REALM

Even large, obvious marine creatures that range widely and are well known and loved may be difficult to protect. Yet through the cooperative and sometimes heroic efforts of people in many countries it has been possible to provide hope for recovery of some. For instance, marine sanctuaries in the United States, such as the Channel Islands and the Gulf of the Farallones, and sanctuaries in Mexico, are providing critical protection for feeding and breeding areas needed by gray whales. But even more creative solutions must be found to ensure the future of wide-ranging fish such as marlin, swordfish,

TIME SEEKERS

NEWCOMERS TO an ancient planet, humans can read much of their history in relicts: some along modern shorelines; others submerged since the last ice age; still others in deep waters far at sea. Thousands of shipwrecks are now accessible that heretofore lay beyond our reach. Marine sanctuaries protect the rich heritage of early human cultures as well as the natural systems that sustained them—and now us. Today more than half the world's population lives within a few miles of a coast, drawn there for reasons that probably appealed to our long-ago ancestors: sustenance, benign climate, aquatic highways allowing access to trade near and far, and perhaps the desire to be near the mesmerizing beauty of living waters.

Bones of coastal dwellers from ages past, opposite, are protected at San Miguel Island, bordering the Channel Islands National Marine Sanctuary. Along the Olympic coast, a shipwreck, above, takes on a new role—as home for enterprising sea creatures.

sailfish, and the highly-prized bluefin tuna, all giant fish that may weigh half a ton or more and swim over entire ocean basins in the course of a year. Within 25 years, up to 90 percent of these once numerous high-seas hunters have been eliminated through sport and commercial fishing. They are magnificent creatures in their own right—as worthy of protection as, say, eagles or panthers.

Regarded by some as the "perfect fish," bluefin tuna migrate over thousands of miles, sometimes traveling as fast as a nuclear submarine. Fine-tuned over millions of years for survival in the open waters, these swift, sleek masters of the ocean might be viewed by aliens as the most highly developed creatures on Earth. Bluefins, after all, have within their own skin all the ingredients needed to communicate with their fellow fish; to navigate effectively without global-positioning devices, satellites, or maps; and to find and capture smaller fish and squid to fuel their energy requirements, sometimes cooperating in a manner suggesting wolves in order to effectively corral their prey.

Certain engineers at the Massachusetts Institute of Technology sigh with envy when they speak of bluefin tuna. They wonder at the fish's retractable dorsal fins, each with a slot into which the fins are withdrawn when minimum drag is desired. Even the pectoral fins that originate just behind the gills have special depressions into which they can be folded precisely, making the form of the fish essentially like that of a torpedo. Torpedoes, actually, have been modeled after tuna, the fish having preceded them by many millions of years. With computers, innovative use of new materials, and considerable thought, a "robotuna" model was constructed at MIT to try to learn the fishes' secrets of effective propulsion. Rarely does a mechanical propeller achieve efficiency greater than 50 percent, but the engineers discovered that by capturing the energy derived from small whirlpools—vortices created as the tuna moves its tail back and forth—efficiency approaches 97 percent.

Nations have joined together in attempts to bring about the recovery of bluefins as they have for certain other far-ranging species, but aside from the difficulties involved in trying to restore greatly depleted populations while still taking large numbers, there is the problem of not knowing much of the basic life-history information. Protection for at least part of a "nursery area" may be provided by the Florida Keys National Marine Sanctuary, judging from the appearance of baby bluefins in the Straits of Florida. But no one has ever seen wild bluefin tuna mating, and not much is known about how long young ones stay near the places where they begin life, nor where they go afterward. It is clear that lucky individuals may live for two or three decades, that well-developed social structure exists among adults, and that their "habitat" is about the size of the world's oceans. To save these giants ultimately means saving the ocean, just as saving wolves requires protection for vast stretches of land.

Tundi Agardy in her thoughtful review, *Marine Protected Areas and Ocean Conservation,* suggests that, all things considered, "The most important role coastal and marine protected areas serve is as a starting point for exploring and delimiting functional linkages in coastal systems . . . ." By themselves, the systems of national parks, national marine sanctuaries, estuarine reserves, wildlife refuges, wilderness areas, and other protected areas cannot ensure that the natural systems that sustain us now will continue to do so in the future—but they help as models of good health, and they help maintain at least representative parts of the asset base that has been building since the solar system was formed. The problem with systems that take 4.6 billion years to develop is nicely articulated by Aldo Leopold in his classic book, *A Sand County Almanac:* "Wilderness is a resource which can shrink but not grow… the creation of new wilderness in the full sense of the word is impossible."

Not long ago, in geological terms, humankind did not have to be so concerned about the number of tuna or whales in the sea, nor the extent of marshes, coral reefs, or kelp forests. Ten thousand years ago, when there were fewer of "us" and more of "them," it was almost reasonable to think that there was little that we could do to significantly modify the natural systems that make the world work as it does. Even so, many scientists believe that the demise of the large megafauna in North America so prominent as the last ice age came to a close probably had much to do with the proficiency of our long-ago predecessors as hunters of wildlife. Edward O. Wilson observes that humankind has, over the ages, relentlessly eliminated "the large, the slow, and the tasty."

No one knows precisely when the first people lived in what is now the United States, but archaeologist Rainer Berger has studied intriguing artifacts from those who early on made a living in the vicinity of California's Channel Islands National Marine Sanctuary. Remains of dwarf mammoths in blackened depressions in the Earth may have been subjected to one of the oldest pit barbeques ever held in southern California—40,000 years ago. At the time, much of the continent was covered with ice, but the offshore islands may have enjoyed a more congenial climate owing to the presence of the surrounding ocean. There is evidence on the Channel Islands as well as in Florida, the Pacific Northwest, and elsewhere along rivers, coasts, and on islands, of the existence of *Homo sapiens* as hunter-gatherers between 10,000 and 15,000 years ago, as the mantle of ice from the end of the Pleistocene epoch gradually retreated.

North America's marine sanctuaries protect much of the rich heritage of early human cultures as well as the natural systems that sustained them then—and us now. Today more than half the world's population lives within a few miles of a coast, drawn there for the same reasons that probably appealed to our predecessors. Twenty miles offshore from the coast of Georgia and 60 feet down at Gray's Reef National Marine Sanctuary, the remains of saber-toothed cats and mastodons have been discovered, and it is possible that humans lived along this ancient shoreline as well. Coastal Georgia is richly endowed with evidence of early human cultures—as recorded by 18th-century naturalist William Bartram—as are the Olympic Coast, Monterey Bay, and Channel Islands Marine Sanctuaries, and American Samoa, which holds Fagatele Bay Marine Sanctuary, is the birthplace of ancient Polynesian culture. Little, however, has been done so far to explore the potential of what may be hidden underwater along now submerged shorelines.

By the time Europeans first arrived in this then-new land, the large animals of the Pleistocene were essentially gone...no more woolly mammoths, giant sloths, or saber-toothed cats, but many of their contemporaries—manatees, panthers, black bears, gopher tortoises, and many more—are still around.

When John Cabot sailed along the North Atlantic coast of North America in 1497, according to Mark Kurlansky, author of *Cod, A Biography of the Fish That Changed the World,* the sea was swarming with fish that could be taken "not only with a net but in baskets let down with a stone...." Well into the 1800s, it was difficult to imagine that we could make major inroads in the abundance of these creatures or other ocean wildlife or harm the ocean in any measurable way, an attitude poetically expressed by Lord Byron nearly two centuries ago when he wrote:

> *Roll on, thou deep and dark blue Ocean—roll!*
> *Ten thousand fleets sweep over thee in vain!*
> *Man marks the earth with ruin—his control*
> *Stops with the shore.*

While there is now plenty of evidence that we can change and are changing the nature of the oceans, when sailors are offshore, there is little doubt about who, ultimately, is in control—and, generally, it is not the humans at the helm. Over the ages, many fleets and thousands of individual ships have become, in effect, artificial reefs along our coastal waters as a consequence of storms or battles or other events that try the ingenuity and the souls of mariners everywhere. In all 12 marine sanctuaries, there are shipwrecks and human artifacts that can contribute significantly to serious questions of our near and distant past.

One of the most famous shipwrecks is the U.S.S. *Monitor,* prototype for a class of Civil War ironclad—a turreted warship that set new standards for naval technology and architecture in the 19th century. The site of the *Monitor* became the first national marine sanctuary established in the United States— in 1975—drawing on the authority provided in legislation enacted in 1972.

The ship's history is dramatic: A few months after surviving a four-hour assault from the Confederate Ironclad, C.S.S. *Virginia,* the *Monitor* succumbed to a severe storm off Cape Hatteras, North Carolina, the part of the eastern seaboard of the United States coastline soberly referred to as "The Graveyard of the Atlantic." There she remains today, at rest in 230 feet of water, a welcome artificial reef for schools of amberjack and occasional large, curious grouper. Although her artifacts can be seen in the nearby Mariner's Museum in Newport News, Virginia, there is still much to learn about the warship—and about preserving her. Because the *Monitor*'s resting place is not easy to access, only trained crews using sophisticated scuba gear, or submersibles, are able to explore the wreck. If proposed research projects are approved, they will yield better understanding of the environment around the warship and its effect on the structure, and ultimately will aid the preservation of other shipwrecks valuable to our heritage.

Humankind cannot effectively control the ocean, but there is no doubt that we have had a profound influence over its nature in the past century. The trick that could serve us well would be to turn the ingenuity that has enabled us to negatively impact the ocean toward positive goals. Peter L. Bernstein observes in *Against the Gods,* "The revolutionary idea that defines the boundary between modern times and the past is the mastery of risk: the notion that the future is more than a whim of the gods and that men and women are not passive before nature.... The ability to define what may happen in the future and to choose among alternatives lies at the heart of contemporary societies."

If a machine existed that could transport us back in time, it might also take us forward to see the consequences of choices we are now making. Modern computers enable us, in a way, to do just that—to help visualize and calculate the consequences of our actions in the next millennium and beyond. What would it mean to us and to the ocean not to have bluefin tuna, anymore, or to exist without whales, having let them slide into extinction? What might be the consequences of consuming the last cod or allowing 350 million years of horseshoe crab lineage to end abruptly in our time, on our watch? No doubt about it, Earth is now and always has been an ongoing "work in progress." The vital issue for us is whether or not we can so manage ourselves that our future will continue far as a vibrant part of the action.

Petroglyph of an orca whale
inscribed into the rocky shoreline
by Ozette natives of Washington's
Olympic coast symbolizes the
respect accorded these great mammals
by peoples of ancient times.
The living reality, at right,
still inspires those fortunate enough
to witness their stunning power,
beauty, and intelligence
in action.

MONITOR
THE FIRST MARINE SANCTUARY

THREE YEARS AFTER legislation was enacted in the United States in 1972 authorizing the establishment of marine sanctuaries, the first—a square mile of ocean surrounding the wreck of the ironclad Civil War ship, U.S.S. *Monitor*—was designated. A few months after surviving a four-hour assault by the Confederate ironclad, C.S.S. *Virginia, Monitor* succumbed to a severe storm off Cape Hatteras, North Carolina, where she remains today, at rest in 230 feet of water. Visitors to the Mariner's Museum in Newport News, Virginia, can see artifacts and learn more about this famous symbol of America's past. Archaeologists are recovering artifacts in an ongoing study of how to preserve this and other underwater shipwrecks.

Researchers, left, use advanced scuba gear, and sometimes submarines, to explore the remains of the U.S.S. Monitor, *a prototype for a class of Civil War ironclad— turreted warships that set new standards for naval technology and architecture in the 19th century. Amberjack, above, are regular visitors to this historic site.*

Poignant reminder of the impact
humankind has had on ocean wildlife,
this Hawaiian monk seal,
most ancient of all seals, is one of
the last of its kind in the world.
Seriously depleted by sealers,
full protection was granted in 1972,
but many now are killed through
entanglement in fishing gear. Babies
call to their mothers with a plaintive
"bahhh," and poet-naturalist
Diane Ackerman, who has observed
them underwater and above,
is fond of listening to their lovely full
repertoire of sounds, "from stuttering
grunts to high-pitched foghorns."
Their future depends on actions
taken—or not taken—while there is
still a chance to save them.

THE FUTURE

MONITOR
THE FIRST MARINE SANCTUARY

THREE YEARS AFTER legislation was enacted in the United States in 1972 authorizing the establishment of marine sanctuaries, the first—a square mile of ocean surrounding the wreck of the ironclad Civil War ship, U.S.S. *Monitor*—was designated. A few months after surviving a four-hour assault by the Confederate ironclad, C.S.S. *Virginia, Monitor* succumbed to a severe storm off Cape Hatteras, North Carolina, where she remains today, at rest in 230 feet of water. Visitors to the Mariner's Museum in Newport News, Virginia, can see artifacts and learn more about this famous symbol of America's past. Archaeologists are recovering artifacts in an ongoing study of how to preserve this and other underwater shipwrecks.

Researchers, left, use advanced scuba gear, and sometimes submarines, to explore the remains of the U.S.S. Monitor, *a prototype for a class of Civil War ironclad— turreted warships that set new standards for naval technology and architecture in the 19th century. Amberjack, above, are regular visitors to this historic site.*

THE FUTURE

THE FUTURE

*The next decade promises to be the most decisive ten years in the history of the planet:
How we proceed will dictate the world's environmental fate.*

WILL STEGER
POLAR EXPLORER

MARINE BIOLOGIST Dan Howard could barely contain his excitement as he reported to me—on shore—about the first leg of the 1999 season of fieldwork for the Sustainable Seas Expeditions: "It's a magical day—perfect conditions for diving. I'm aboard the NOAA ship *McArthur* and Tom Laidig is 104 feet below in *Deep Worker*, rhapsodizing about what he sees. The Farallon Islands are a perfect backdrop for two gray whales now spouting about ten feet off the bow. The sea is alive with krill swarming in huge masses. A school of rockfish just exploded from below in a frenzied boil, driving the krill right out of the water. Hundreds of gulls are working the surface; they swirl, circle, then pounce on the krill like cats."

Listening to Dan, I was mindful that gray whales, and even rockfish, might be just wistful memories but for a widespread change of heart—and of policies. Fortunately for the whales, and for us, a new ethic emerged in this century that enabled us to step back from the brink of permanent loss of many of the nation's valuable natural assets. Caring people years ago made the difference between whether or not the seas of their future—our present—could be rich with whales, birds, and fish such as Dan now observed.

In the 1950s the inherent value—and vulnerability—of the wild ocean had a champion in Rachel Carson, whose ocean trilogy included the classic, *The Sea Around Us.* In a 1953 letter to the *Washington Post,* she observed, "The

A powerful symbol of resilience and hope, this elephant seal near
Monterey, California, is a descendant of a once thriving population reduced to less
than a hundred by sealers in the late 1800s. Now numbering in the
thousands, these seals compatibly share space with people along
much of North America's West Coast.

PRECEDING PAGES: *New frontiers for exploration await in*
the depths below, home for most of life on Earth—and the cornerstone of Earth's
life support. Protection for the wild ocean systems that sustain us
is vital for present and future prosperity.

real wealth of the nation lies in the resources of the Earth: soil, water, forests, minerals, and wildlife. To utilize them for present needs while insuring their preservation for future generations requires a delicately balanced and continuing program, based on the most extensive research." A modern champion for wild systems is Jane Lubchenco, who spearheads a program Carson would applaud, "based on the most extensive research." With funding from the Packard Foundation in cooperation with four universities, it explores over years the nature of one of the nation's most influential ocean systems—the California Current. With strong support from many scientific colleagues, she makes a compelling case for the need to fully protect at least 20 percent of the ocean by 2020.

Marine scientist John Ogden suggests that the entire Exclusive Economic Zone be subdivided for varying degrees of protection. The concept has proven viable in Australia, where thousands of square miles of ocean have been zoned for multiple uses. This idea is now being explored on a smaller scale, in the Florida Keys Sanctuary. A thoughtful proposal for having internationally respected marine protected areas in the open sea beyond the jurisdiction of individual nations has been advanced by Maxine McCloskey, one of the few who has addressed the difficult issue of how to protect wide-ranging species. International involvement is vital, even for protection of national interests, given the continuity of the ocean as a fully connected, global system. The World Conservation Union recently inventoried some 1,300 places, worldwide, that enjoy protection.

In the United States by 1990, considerable interest was growing about the role marine sanctuaries and other protected areas could have in restoring and safeguarding the ocean. A few areas had already been named, but resources were slim—3 million dollars for the entire program. Monitoring and assessment programs advanced by NOAA scientists Nancy Foster, Charles Ehler, Dan Basta, and others were starting to pay off, however, drawing attention to the importance of new protective measures. The Center for Marine Conservation provided vital sustained support, from organizing grassroots endorsement to keeping members of Congress informed about the issues at stake. Nancy Foster summed up the need: "Earth is a marine habitat."

As chief scientist of NOAA in the early 1990s, I took part in many meetings aimed at expanding the sanctuaries. Especially *(continued on page 211)*

Veiled with spray, a humpback leaps from the sea in the cold northern end of its range, in Alaska. Here vital food sources abound during summer months; come winter, the whale will travel to warm seas.

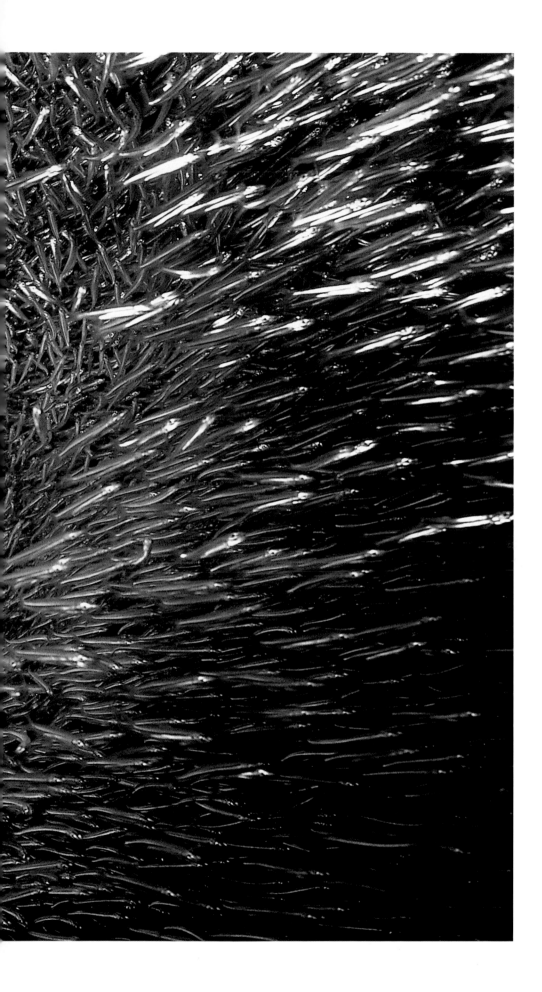

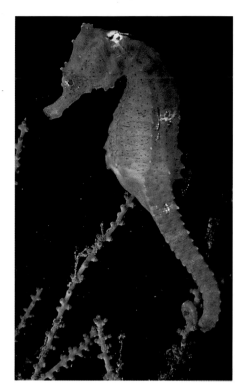

The web of life in motion, a hungry snapper, left, targets glassy minnows who in turn feed on small crustaceans. Above, a seahorse clings to a soft coral in the Florida Keys National Marine Sanctuary. A growing market for these appealing little fish as curios and medicinals increases the urgency of having sanctuaries if they are to grace the oceans of the future.

FOLLOWING PAGES: *Sky and sea merge with a rush of wings and spray as an American bald eagle scoops sustenance from productive waters. The survival and well-being of these elegant birds—and of all life on Earth, including humankind— depends on healthy seas.*

Seagrass meadows in the Big Bend area along
the northwestern coast of Florida, with their thriving
populations of shrimp, below, juvenile fish,
and numerous other creatures, link directly to the coral
reefs and other ocean ecosystems in the Florida Keys.
Like miniature rain forests, only wetter,
undersea gardens, at right, release large amounts
of oxygen into the atmosphere. They also provide food
and shelter for the young of numerous species that
later range widely. Protection for these highly
productive meadows would help ensure the good health
of the Gulf of Mexico and the ocean beyond.

encouraging was a report of a special commission chaired by Frank Potter, a hero to many for his part in bringing about the original legislation authorizing marine sanctuaries. Carleton Ray, pioneer in developing ecosystem-based plans for marine-protected areas, provided key guidance. "The Potter Report," as it became known, envisioned by the year 2000 "a comprehensive and integrated system of the nation's most significant marine areas…based on ecologically sound, well-researched principles of resource protection and sustainable use…and as well on improving public understanding of the nation's marine heritage…."

With 12 sanctuaries now in place, we have a good start toward achieving that vision, but dozens of sites under consideration for many years have been put on hold, while the need for protective measures becomes more urgent. Among the national treasures given high marks for protection is a sweeping underwater prairie of seagrasses, limestone reefs, and open sandy areas encompassing hundreds of square miles of productive, sunlit waters—the Big Bend area in the eastern Gulf of Mexico. Other places include Oceanographer Canyon offshore from Massachusetts; the Point of Hatteras, North Carolina, where the warm Gulf Stream current collides with deep, cold currents; coral reefs in the U.S. Virgin Islands; sites in the Great Lakes of historically valuable shipwrecks; and pristine areas along the coast of Alaska. Among many deep-water locations are Pioneer Seamount near California's Farallon Islands, and hydrothermal vents at Gorda Ridge 6,000 feet down, off the Oregon coast.

There are many other places, some known only by shadowy sonar images. The situation before us is comparable to what it would be to create a plan for North America as it was a thousand years ago, knowing what we now know. Our challenge is to be wise about the fate of that other, submerged America.

At the National Oceans Conference in Monterey, in 1998, First Lady Hillary Rodham Clinton spoke for many when she said, "I think it's important for all of us to pause and consider what it is we want to leave to future generations, and how we'll honor the past and imagine the future and give gifts to those who will live their lives in the 21st century." There is a window in time, now, when we could forever lose a priceless ocean wilderness heritage—or develop the foundation for an enduring legacy of natural and historic treasures, an inspired gift from the 20th century to all who follow.

The nation's inland "seas," the Great Lakes harbor a wealth of life and history, including the ribs and remains of many historic shipwrecks such as this one, at rest along the shore of Lake Huron, in Presque Isle County, Michigan.

The future of life in the sea,
from creatures such as this Pacific
white-sided dolphin to
the smallest microbe, relate
to actions we take to protect the
vital systems that sustain
them—and us.

◇ CHANNEL ISLANDS

AT THIS KEY NESTING SITE for endangered brown pelicans, visitors can see a vast range of creatures, from tiny anemones to massive blue whales. The mix of warm and cool currents allows this variety of life, which includes elephant seals, dolphins, blue sharks, and garibaldi. Along the shore, historic shipwrecks and ancient Chumash Indian sites are preserved. The Sea Center, a marine aquarium and educational facility, features exhibits, lectures, volunteer programs, and curricula for teachers. A research vessel gives on-site assistance. Contact: 113 Harbor Way, Santa Barbara, CA 93109 (tel: 805-966-7107)

◇ GULF OF THE FARALLONES

OFF THE SHORE of San Francisco, the Gulf of the Farallones Sanctuary features nurseries and grounds for feeding some 30 species of marine mammals and 15 species of seabirds. The Farallon Island chain is a wildlife refuge where visitors find the largest concentration of breeding seabirds in the continental U. S. On the mainland coast, the public discovers shipwrecks, fossil beds, lagoons, estuaries, and beaches. Volunteer and educational programs include BeachWatch, Sea Camp, and teacher curricula development. Contact: Fort Mason, Building #201, San Francisco, CA 94123 (tel: 415-561-6622)

◇ FLORIDA KEYS

BEST KNOWN FOR ITS CORAL REEFS, the Florida Keys ecosystem supports one of the most diverse groupings of marine plants and animals in North America. Its fringing mangroves, seagrass meadows, hardbottom regions, and bank reefs entice millions of visitors yearly. See angelfish, spiny lobsters, grouper, brain coral, and sea fans. Historic shipwrecks and lighthouses beckon. A plan to protect the Keys' 220-mile arc of reefs involves people through interpretive tours, class-and-field programs, Team OCEAN volunteer effort, and research activities. Contact: P.O. Box 500368, Marathon, FL 33050 (tel: 305-743-2437)

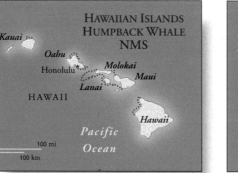

◇ FLOWER GARDEN BANKS

A PREMIERE DIVING DESTINATION that harbors the northernmost coral reefs in the United States, Flower Garden Banks, with nearby Stetson Bank, forms a unique sanctuary. From the ocean floor 100 miles off Louisiana and Texas rise the three salt domes, upon which grow gardens of coral and sponges. Through them swim manta rays, hammerhead sharks, loggerhead turtles, blennies, and barracudas. The sanctuary offers classroom and shipboard presentations, teacher workshops, research cruises, fellowships, fish, turtle, and coral surveys. Contact: 216 W. 26th St. Suite 104, Bryan, TX 77803 (tel: 409-779-2705)

◇ HAWAIIAN ISLANDS

NEARLY TWO-THIRDS of the estimated 6,000 North Pacific humpback whales mate and calve in this sanctuary—the only reserve dedicated to one species. The shallow warm waters rich with coral reefs also support Hawaiian monk seals, spinner dolphins, green sea turtles, and triggerfish. The sanctuary is crucial to the long-term recovery of the endangered humpbacks. The sanctuary has classroom and on-site presentations, community events, support for whale behavior studies, and volunteer and intern programs. Contact: 726 S. Kihei Rd., Kihei, HI 96753 (tel: 808-879-2818)

◇ MONTEREY BAY

THE LARGEST MARINE sanctuary spans some 5,300 square miles off the coast of central California. Here thrives the nation's greatest diversity of habitats: from rocky shores and kelp forests to a two-mile-deep ocean canyon. Equally diverse is the marine life, which includes sea otters, gray whales, and market squids. The sanctuary features exhibits, lectures, a volunteer program, teacher workshops, and research activities. It works closely with the nearby Monterey Bay Aquarium (tel: 831-648-4888). Contact the sanctuary at 299 Foam Street, Monterey, CA 93940 (tel: 831-647-4201)

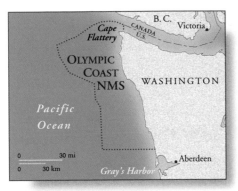

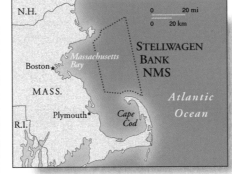

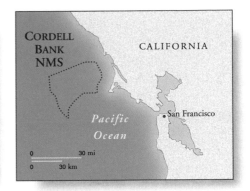

◇ OLYMPIC COAST

OFF THE RUGGED OLYMPIC PENINSULA, 3,310 square miles of sanctuary waters cover much of the continental shelf and protect the habitat for one of the most diverse marine mammal faunas in North America. Here northern sea otters, humpback and gray whales, and dolphins abound. The sanctuary hosts critical breeding colonies of cormorants; bald eagles also can be seen here. Cultural assets are shipwrecks, lighthouses, and local Native Americans sharing their ancient heritage. Activities range from ecotourism programs to archaeological and biological research. Contact: 138 West First Street, Port Angeles, WA 98362 (tel: 360-457-6622)

◇ STELLWAGEN BANK

RETREATING GLACIERS during the last ice age deposited coarse sand and gravel off the coast of Massachusetts, creating the bank. Over it flows an upwelling of nutrient-rich waters from the Gulf of Maine, making for high productivity and a multilayered food web from phytoplankton to northern right whales. The nearby New England Aquarium (tel: 617-973-5200) offers numerous exhibits of sealife. Workshops train teachers and other professionals. Programs include outreach seminars and student research with the University of Connecticut. Contact: 175 Edward Foster Rd., Scituate, MA 02066 (tel: 781-545-8026)

◇ CORDELL BANK

A SEAMOUNT 60 MILES northwest of San Francisco lies in a propitious path, where oceanic conditions and undersea topography together create a productive environment. The prevailing California Current flows southward along the coast and combines with the upwelling of nutrient-rich, deep-ocean waters to stimulate growth of organisms at all levels of the food web. Here thrive krill, salmon, rockfish, whales, porpoises, shearwaters, and albatrosses. The center hosts teacher workshops, whale studies, and pelagic surveys. Contact: Fort Mason, Building #201, San Francisco, CA 94123 (tel: 415-561-6622).

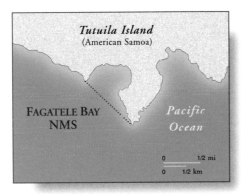

◇ FAGATELE BAY

NESTLED WITHIN AN ERODED volcanic crater on the island of Tutuila, in American Samoa, this coral reef ecosystem is in recovery. Nearly 200 species of coral, heavily attacked by crown-of-thorns starfish in the late 1970s, are being aided in their comeback by programs at the sanctuary center: a summer camp, a school and village outreach, a coral-reef habitat survey, and a resource recovery survey. Visitors view blacktip reef sharks and giant clams. They learn of the 3,000-year-old Polynesian culture, which has origins there. Contact: P.O. Box 4318, Pago Pago, American Samoa 96799 (tel: 011-684-633-7354)

◇ GRAY'S REEF

ITS DIVERSITY OF MARINE LIFE makes Gray's Reef one of the most popular diving and sport fishing destinations along the Georgia coast. It also is noted as one of the largest near-shore sandstone reefs in the southeastern U.S. Discover its habitats of calcareous sandstone, of tropical/temperate reefs, and of species including the northern right whale, loggerhead sea turtle, grouper, angelfish, black sea bass, and barrel sponge. Programs include community seminars, curriculum planning, research projects, and archaeological surveys. Contact: 10 Ocean Science Circle, Savannah, GA 31411 (tel: 912-598-2345)

◇ MONITOR

THE NATION'S FIRST MARINE SANCTUARY was designated in 1975. It thrives in a one-square-mile area around the wreck of the U.S.S. *Monitor,* the Civil War ironclad that sank off the coast of North Carolina in 1862. Today it is an artificial reef frequented by myriad species: amberjack, scad, corals, and sea urchins. *Monitor*'s location on the seafloor precludes most people from visiting. However, outreach programs bring the site to the public. Research on its environment and history are under way. Contact: The Mariner's Museum, 100 Museum Drive, Newport News, VA 23606 (tel: 757-599-3122)

With care, the nation's oceans will be safe havens
for these California fur seals, their descendants, and ours,
for many millennia to come.

NOTES ON CONTRIBUTORS

DR. SYLVIA EARLE is a marine biologist, author, lecturer, and ocean explorer. She is the National Geographic Society's Explorer-in-Residence for 1998 through 2002. As part of the Sustainable Seas Expeditions launched in 1998 with Society support, Earle will dive in all 12 U.S. marine sanctuaries. Called "Her Deepness" by the *New York Times,* she was in 1998 named the first "Hero for the Planet" by *Time* magazine. Earle has a B.S. from Florida State University and a Ph.D. from Duke University, as well as numerous honorary doctorates. When not underwater, Earle lives in Oakland, California.

WOLCOTT HENRY is president of the Curtis and Edith Munson Foundation, an organization that supports marine conservation in North America. He is also an underwater photographer who has explored marine areas all over the world, including Brazil, Papua New Guinea, the Galápagos Islands, Hawaii, and the continental United States. His photographs are often used by nonprofit groups to communicate the importance of the ocean. He lives in Washington, D.C.

DEDICATION:
*To those who knew and cared enough to
protect the wild ocean in times past so that there can be
a wild ocean in the future.*

ACKNOWLEDGMENTS

Thanks are due to many who have made this book possible, first and foremost, our friends and colleagues in the National Geographic Book Division, especially Barbara Brownell, Tom Powell, Suez Corrado, and Mary Jennings, with whom we worked closely throughout. Nina Hoffman and Will Gray provided valuable oversight, and most important, believed in the vision *Wild Ocean* intends to portray. We are grateful to the many people who shared their thoughts about the ocean for this book and regret we could not include all the wonderful wealth of material submitted. We appreciate the thoughtful input from Francesca Cava, Linda Glover, Elizabeth Taylor, and Gale Mead, who made constructive comments on various drafts, and also want to thank friends at NOAA, the World Wildlife Fund, and the Center for Marine Conservation, especially Jack Sobel, for supplying valuable resource materials. Also, we want to express our love and thanks to all who have fostered within us, and for the world, the sense of caring we have tried to portray—parents, family, friends, and many fish, whales, squid, and other fine creatures of the sea.

—*Sylvia Earle and Wolcott Henry*

The Book Division is also grateful to Justin Kenney, NOAA National Marine Sanctuaries; Ken Peterson, public relations manager Monterey Bay Aquarium; Tundi Agardy, Conservation International; and all the managers and superintendents for the national marine sanctuaries. In addition, we thank Lyn Clement for her careful reading of the final manuscript.

Composition for this book by the National Geographic Society Book Division. Color separations by Quad Graphics, Martinsburg, West Virginia. Printed and bound by R.R. Donnelley & Sons, Willard, Ohio. Dust jacket printed by Miken, Inc., Cheektowaga, N.Y.

PHOTOGRAPHIC CREDITS

Introduction: 1, Phillip Colla. 2-3, Wolcott Henry. 4 (t), Brandon D. Cole. 4 (ctr), Flip Nicklin/Minden Pictures. 4 (b), Flip Nicklin. 5 (t), Flip Nicklin. 5 (ctr), Kip Evans. 5 (b), Stephen Frink/Waterhouse. 6, Clay H. Wiseman. 10-11, David Doubilet. 17, Clay H. Wiseman. **The Mammalian Connection:** 18-19, Brandon D. Cole. 21, Doug Perrine/Innerspace Visions. 24-25, Doug Perrine/ Innerspace Visions. 26-27, Michael S. Nolan/Innerspace Visions. 27, Lori Mazzuca. 30-31, Brandon D. Cole. 32-33, Deborah Glockner-Ferrari/Center for Whale Studies. Photos taken under scientific permits granted by National Marine Fisheries Service and State of Hawaii. 34-35, Phillip Cola. 35 (t), Flip Nicklin. 35 (b), Peter Howorth/MoYung Productions. 36-37, Doug Perrine/Innerspace Visions. 40-41, Bob Cranston/Innerspace Visions. 41, Dan Polin/"Light, Words & Music." 46-47, George H.H. Huey. 48, Bob Cranston. 49 (t), Richard Herrmann. 49 (b), Frans Lanting/Minden Pictures. 50-51, James A. Sugar/Black Star. **In Warm Waters:** 52-53, Flip Nicklin/Minden Pictures. 55, David Doubilet. 58-59, David Doubilet. 60-61, Dave Fleetham/Pacific Stock. 64-65, Stephen Frink/Waterhouse. 66-67(both), Wolcott Henry. 68-69, Franklin J. Viola. 69, Flip Nicklin/Minden Pictures. 70-71 (both), Wolcott Henry. 72-73, Bianca Lavies. 73, Stephen Frink/Waterhouse. 74-75, Clay H. Wiseman. 80, James Watt/Waterhouse. 81 (t), Karen Angle. 81 (b), Wolcott Henry. 84-85, Kip Evans. 85 (both), Wolcott Henry. 86-87, Flip Nicklin. 88-89, Frans Lanting/Minden Pictures. **In Cold Waters:** 90-91, Flip Nicklin. 93, Flip Nicklin/Minden Pictures. 96-97, Jack Dykinga. 98, Andrew J. Martinez. 99, Courtesy Cordell Expeditions. 100-101, Jonathan S. Blair. 102-103, Jeff Foott. 107, Kevin Schafer. 108-109, James D. Watt. 110-111, Chuck Davis. 111 (t), Kevin McDonnell. 111 (ctr), Wolcott Henry. 111(b), Stuart Westmorland. 112 (t), Chuck Davis. 112 (b), Wolcott Henry. 113, Howard Hall. 118 (t), Jonathan S. Blair. 118 (b), Emory Kristof. 119, Norbert Wu. 120, George I. Matsumoto/MBARI. 120-121, Richard Herrmann. 121, Kevin A.Raskoff/MBARI. 125, Richard Herrmann. 126 -127, George H.H. Huey. **A New Way of Looking At Fish:** 128-129, Flip Nicklin.131, Stephen Frink/Waterhouse. 134-135, Jonathan S. Blair. 138-139 (both), Wolcott Henry. 142-143, Brian Parker/Tom Stack & Assoc. 143, Medford Taylor. 144-145, Wolcott Henry. 146, Bob Young. 150, Wolcott Henry. 151, Stephen Frink/Waterhouse. 152 (tl), Howard Hall. 152 (bl), Wolcott Henry. 152 (tr), Masa Ushioda/Innerspace Visions. 152 (br), Michele Hall. 152-153, Richard Herrmann. 153, Wolcott Henry. 157, Jesse Cancelmo. 158, Jonathan S. Blair. 158-159, Nate O. Johnson/Orion Photos. 160-161, David Doubilet. 162-163, Richard Herrmann. **The Sweep of Time:** 164-165, Kip Evans. 167, Bob Cranston. 170-171, Eleonara de Sabata. 172, Frans Lanting. 176-177, Kevin Schafer. 178-179 (all), Wolcott Henry. 180-181, Stuart Westmorland/Tony Stone Images. 182, Wolcott Henry.183, Brandon D. Cole. 186, Frank S. Balthis. 186-187, Frans Lanting/Minden Pictures. 192, Fred Hirschmann. 192-193, Gerry Ellis/ENP Images. 194-195 (both), Rod Farb. 196-197, David B. Fleetham/Innerspace Visions. **The Future:** 198-199, Stephen Frink/Waterhouse. 201, John Cang. 203, Stuart Westmorland/Tony Stone Images. 204-205, Stephen Frink/Waterhouse. 205, Doug Perrine/Innerspace Visions. 206-207, Jim Simmen/Tony Stone Images. 208-209, Heather Dine/Florida Keys National Marine Sanctuary. 209, Bianca Lavies. 210, Gary Alan Nelson. 212-213, Stuart Westmorland. 216-217, Tim Thompson.

ADDITIONAL READING

Tundi Agardy, *Marine Protected Areas and Ocean Conservation;* Rachel Carson, *The Sea Around Us.* Douglas Chadwick, "Blue Refuges," NATIONAL GEOGRAPHIC, March 1998; Sylvia Earle, *Sea Change: A Message of the Oceans;* G. Kelleher, C. Bleakly, S. Wells, *A Global Representation System of Marine Protection (4 vols.);* Aldo Leopold, *A Sand County Almanac;* Carl Safina, *Song for the Blue Ocean;* Charles Seaborn, *Underwater Wilderness;* NOAA National Marine Sanctuaries, *A Tour of the Sanctuaries,* and *Accomplishments Report, 1998;* Eds. Woods Hole Oceanographic Institution, "Marine Protected Areas," *Oceanus,* Fall 1993.

INDEX

Boldface indicates illustrations.

WILD OCEAN
AMERICA'S PARKS UNDER THE SEA
By Sylvia A. Earle and Wolcott Henry

Published by the National Geographic Society

John M. Fahey, Jr. *President and Chief Executive Officer*

Gilbert M. Grosvenor *Chairman of the Board*

Nina D. Hoffman *Senior Vice President*

Prepared by the Book Division

William R. Gray *Vice President and Director*

Charles Kogod *Assistant Director*

Barbara A. Payne *Editorial Director and Managing Editor*

David Griffin *Design Director*

Staff for this Book

Barbara Brownell *Editor*

Suez Kehl Corrado *Art Director*

Tom Powell *Illustrations Editor*

Mary Jennings *Researcher*

Carl Mehler *Director of Maps*

NG Maps and Joseph F. Ochlak *Map Research*

Michelle H. Picard *Map Production*

R. Gary Colbert *Production Director*

Lewis R. Bassford *Production Project Manager*

Richard Wain *Production Manager*

Sharon Kocsis Berry *Illustrations Assistant*

Peggy J. Candore *Assistant to the Director*

Kevin G. Craig Dale-Marie Herring *Staff Assistants*

Elisabeth MacRae-Bobynskj *Indexer*

Manufacturing and Quality Management

George V. White *Director*

John T. Dunn *Associate Director*

Vincent P. Ryan Gregory Storer *Managers*

James J. Sorensen *Budget Analyst*

Library of Congress ⌶⌿ Data:

Earle, Sylvia A., 1935-
    Wild ocean : America's parks under the sea / Sylvia A. Earle,
Wolcott Henry.
        p.   cm.
    Includes index.
        ISBN 0-7922-7471-7 (alk. paper). — ISBN 0-7922-7469-5 (dlx : alk.
paper)
        1. Marine parks and reserves—United States. 2. Marine organisms-
-United States. I. Henry, Wolcott. II. Title.
QH91.75.U6E18 1999
333.78'3'0973099162—dv21   99-26847
                                                          ⌶⌿